Project Risk Management

The Most Important Methods and Tools
for Successful Projects

ROLAND WANNER

Published by:
Proconis 2013

Disclaimer
This publication is designed to provide competent and reliable information regarding the subject matter covered. However it is not intended as a substitute for legal or other professional services. Readers are urged to consult a variety of sources and professional expert assistance. While every effort has been made to make this book accurate, it may contain typographical and content errors.
The information expressed herein is the opinion of the author, and is not intended to reflect upon any particular person or company. The author and publisher shall have no responsibility or liability with respect to any losses or damage caused, or alleged to be caused, by the information or application of the information contained in this book.
For any questions about the book or the author, please refer to contact details at:
www.pm-risk.com

Version 1.0: March 2013

Content

Preface

. . . .

There's hardly an area of activity in project management in which demand, acceptance, and practice greatly differ from the way it does in risk management. In this book, you will find out more about the many different reasons for this. An important point, however, is that many stakeholders have not recognized some basic facts: Projects collapse under risks! This statement seems trivial at first glance but it is not so obvious for most stakeholders. Upon closer consideration, you would recognize that risks brought imbalance to your project or steered it into a catastrophe. It was risks that were not recognized, ignored, not taken seriously, underestimated or simply neglected.

Do not wait until the next Project Crisis!

How much tension and excitement can you handle during your project? If you do not practice risk management, then I promise you that you will experience a highly interesting project! Something will always be going on and you will never get some peace. It may still be exciting to correct problems on multiple project areas in the beginning – but as time goes by, you will be so stressed that you would rather throw everything down. Do you really want it to come this far?

The next project crisis will definitely come again. Do not remain idle; you should instead practice precaution through active risk management! Risks belong to projects as does air to breath. Nevertheless, risks are gladly being ignored. You act in the illusion of safety of numbers and plan values, based on which all makes the best impression. Furthermore, there are short-term individual interests, politics, and greediness – everything that distorts the clear view of the actual circumstances. No one wants to know anything about risks once the pressure is large enough. You fall into the role of the worrier too fast. "Something like this just happens every now and then," is usually the standard comment. That sounds like irrevocable fate, as if success or failure of a project is somehow predetermined.

Risks do not arise on their own; there are reasons, which usually make themselves known so you can do something about them. Managing risks does not mean to react to random events without a plan and then wait and see what happens. Rather, it means to systematically and actively search for risks and then seize the appropriate actions against them.

What is often forgotten is that risk management is not only concerned with dangers but also with opportunities. Risks are directly connected with opportunities. If you factor the opportunities in to the risk disclosure, you are additionally increasing the chances for your project's success.

Professional project risk management is, unfortunately, a very rarely constant in business, and if it is available, it is only half-heartedly put into practice. This has many reasons: an important reason is the business culture and the maturity of project management. A person, who avows to risk management, has to reduce acceptance obstacles, want a culture of openness, transparency and team spirit and not view risk management as a contradiction. If you practice risk management in your projects as project manager, then you have to act out of conviction. If it doesn't seem to make sense to you, then you should leave it at that. It will only become an alibi exercise.

Don't wait for the next project crisis. Pursue prevention through active risk management! This book is packed with essential knowledge how to successfully apply risk management in projects. You will receive hands-on instructions and tips that you can immediately implement in your project. With this knowledge, you can make your projects even more successful and protect your project life from many problems.

This book describes the most important methods and tools how to successfully apply risk management in projects in a practical and easy-to-use way. You will receive hands-on instructions and tips that you can immediately implement in your project. The terminology described herein follows the generally accepted PMBOK® Guide Fifth Edition. With this knowledge, you can make your projects even more successful and protect your project life from many problems.

I wish you good luck with your next project, but don't rely on it alone!

Introduction

● ●

Why do Projects and Risks belong together?

Wouldn't it be nice if projects didn't have any risks? It would make the project life for a lot of project managers easy – "Easy Project Life!". You could spare a lot of work, stress and surprises. Unfortunately, projects are afflicted with risks by nature. The following project characteristics therefore have a strong influence on the risk level of a project:

- **Uniqueness:** The project includes at least some elements that have never been done before.
- **Complexity:** Diverse associated requirements in the technical or commercial area, at interfaces or in organizational areas.
- **Assumptions and Constraints:** The future development, both pronounced (open) and implicit (hidden) could prove to be false.
- **People:** The project team and senior management, customers, suppliers and subcontractors are all unpredictable to a certain extent.
- **Requirements of Stakeholders:** Their expectations and goals can change, overlap, or sometimes contradict.
- **Changes:** Each project changes and moves slightly from the known presence in an unknown future.
- **Environment:** Both, the internal, organizational environment, and the external environment, in which changes occur, can often not be controlled by the project.

These project characteristics belong to the nature of all projects and cannot be eliminated without changing the project itself. A project, for example, which isn't unique, has no restrictions, doesn't concern any people, and doesn't generate any changes, would, in fact, not be a project anymore! Even the attempt to remove the risk elements of a project would turn it into something else and it probably wouldn't be a project in the classical sense anymore. Provocatively said: "No risk, no opportunity!"

Projects are carried out to generate a benefit. At the same time, you are accepting the associated risks and trying to master these. It is, therefore,

I would be careful if your project didn't have any risks!

impossible to imagine a project without risks. The "Zero Risk Project" is a contradiction in itself. Effective risk management is therefore vital for the success of a project.

Can you even Manage Risks?

Something is not OK with the word "risk management" in my opinion. If you have engaged yourself with risks for a certain amount of time, then ask yourself why this method is actually called "risk management". There must be a misunderstanding. You are probably asking yourself why I am coming to this statement? Keep reading and you'll find out.

In today's economic world, you strive to skillfully manage five types of resources: capital, physical things, people, information, and time. That usually works well, except for the part about time. Is time management possible? Time, as an invisible resource, continually elapses – no one gets more than the other. The clock cannot be turned back or accelerated; therefore, time cannot be managed. We can only manage "ourselves", according to the time. It's quite similar to risk management.

Can you manage risks? You can answer this question yourself after a short explanation of what a risk is. A risk is an uncertainty, which lies in the future and may or may not possibly occur.

You cannot manage risks, but rather measures

If this uncertainty occurs, it becomes a certainty, which means a problem. This uncertainty (the risk) is invisible and therefore not capable of being seized. Can you manage something like that?

You cannot manage risks! However, you can take actions to affect the probability or the effect of the risk. These actions can then be managed through planning, monitoring, and control. You can't influence (manage) the risk that it could rain. However, you can manage actions that could reduce or avoid the possible damage caused by the rain by packing an umbrella or by closing the roof of your convertible.

Threat or Opportunity?

Upon first glance, risks may seem to be the opposite of security; however, this perception falls short. Especially from the business point of view, uncertainties usually contain a positive element. If, for example, you react to market risks, it's also always related to a possible realization of market opportunities. The term "risk" therefore, has to be taken away from an entirely negative interpretation and has to be added to the opportunity aspect. A risk is always a threat and an opportunity at once. The Chinese symbol for crisis is a combination of "danger" and "opportunity". This is no coincidence; a crisis always offers – according to Buddhists, but above all Chinese understanding - the chance for a fresh start. – –

Figure 1: Crisis – Danger or Opportunity?

Are You Risk-Averse or Rather Risk Seeking?

The attitude towards risks is different from person to person. The spectrum reaches from risk-averse (uncomfortable with uncertainty) to risk tolerant (no special reaction) up to risk seeking (uncertainty is welcomed). The attitude towards risks has a substantial influence on the risk management activities. A risk-averse product innovation team does just as little good as a risk seeking nuclear safety inspector.

As you have noticed, risks not only include uncertainties, which could have negative consequences, but also uncertainties with positive consequences. Risks also have a direct connection to profits. Simply said: the more risks a business is willing to take for its projects, the bigger the possible profit. Now, we have to weigh how much risk are we willing to take and what is the potential opportunity in return?

Whoever doesn't take any risks will definitely stand still! The will to take a risk depends directly on the possibility to generate an appropriate opportunity out of it. A business should encourage responsible risk-taking and not punish setbacks. Only when it comes to personal safety is risk-taking not an option!

> *Renaults' chef designer, Le Quément, to the new adventurous design of the Renault luxury models: "Of course we are taking risk, but it would be even more of a risk not to risk anything at all."*

What is your Risk Attitude?

Organizations and stakeholders are willing to accept varying degrees of risk depending on their risk attitude. These risk attitudes are driven by perception, tolerance and other biases, which should be explicit wherever possible. Risk responses reflect an organizations perceived balance between risk taking and risk avoidance. The risk attitude of both, the organization and the stakeholders may be influenced by a number of factors, which are, according to the PMBOK, broadly classified into these three themes:

Risk appetite, which is the degree of uncertainty an entity is willing to take on, into anticipation of a reward.

Risk tolerance, which is the degree, amount or value of risk that an organization or individual will withstand.

Risk threshold, which refers to measures along the level of uncertainty or the level of impact at which a stakeholder may have a specific interest. Below that risk threshold, the organization will accept the risk; above it will not be tolerated.

Why Risk Management?

The Significance of Risk Management for Businesses

The topic of risk management is becoming more important for businesses because of the strategic importance of projects, especially because projects are becoming more demanding and complex. On the other hand, large projects always mean a bigger financial risk for companies.

Identifying opportunities and risks early on and being capable of approaching these actively and as a whole are key success factors of a risk-aware management in today's market activities. The opportunity and danger potential will increase by the rapidly changing technology and the opening of markets all around the world. At the same time, changing economic and social conditions are a huge challenge for many businesses.

The topic of risk management has gained in importance in the last few years, particularly in the eyes of the legislators and the regulatory authorities. Ever since the accounting scandals during the "New Economy" in the USA and Europe between 1999 and 2004, the topic of Corporate Governance is being discussed more strongly once again.

Since 1 May 1998, corporations in Germany are encouraged to establish a company-wide risk monitoring system (§91 Paragraph 2 of AktG) by law of the "Corporate Sector and Supervision Transparency Act" (Gesetz zur Kontrolle und Transparenz im Unternehmensbereich – KonTraG – similar to Sarbanes Oxley Act) for the minimization of risks (now extended and effectively superseded by Basel III), which are recommendations on banking laws and regulations. With the new capital resources agreement of the Basel Committee on Banking Supervision, new conditions are being created, which are incentives to support further development of risk management in the banking sector.

Is poor project management a crime? The answer could be "yes", according to the Sarbanes-Oxley Act. After the various financial scandals became public, the US Congress passed – a little hastily – the Sarbanes-Oxley Act (SOX) at the end of July 2002. This act places every

Poor project management could be a crime!

CFO and CEO and the depiction of the real financial condition of the company into the spotlight. A central point in the Sarbanes-Oxley Act is the independence of the internal audit, but, most importantly, are the new strict corporate governance rules.

These new rules are laws, which force you to place serious risk management in projects. Poor or inexistent risk management in projects will always take revenge – by law!

At the end of the year 2008, a huge financial- and economic crisis broke out. Many banks, especially in the USA, went bankrupt or had to be supported by the federal government. The risk management systems of the banks had obviously fallen prey to the greed of the investment and mortgage banks. The effects of this crisis on the global economy will remain to be seen in the next years. The prospects are not really good at the moment (end of 2009).

Even your Kids do Risk Management

Risks and risk management are becoming more important to your company; however, this is nothing new to us. Do you remember your childhood? Infants don't know what a risk is yet. We often have to save them from imminent dangers and constantly remind them what could happen if...

As of a certain age, each of us practices risk management – consciously or unconsciously. As a child, we learn very early to be aware of possible risks and unconsciously consider these as time goes by. When we cross a street, we look to the left first and then to the right and only then do we cross the street. Who among us would take a risk to cross a street with his/her eyes closed? The possibility that, just then, a car would drive by when we are crossing the street is not small.

Another example for conscious risk management is vacation planning. When you are going on vacation by car, you are accurately preparing yourself and making a detailed plan. During travel planning, you are asking yourself what all could happen during the vacation. Then, you take corresponding measures so that these risks do not arise or, if they do arise, they will not

Everyone does risk management upon planning his/her vacation.

cause large financial or physical damages. That is why you have a spare canister of fuel in the trunk, have completed travel insurance, and have taken the car to get serviced before the trip.

With the passing of years, we continually learn something new. We "mature" and can more clearly evaluate the environment and behavioral patterns, whereas with projects, we haven't learned much in the last 30 years. Many projects still fail or are cancelled. Why? You will learn more about this on the next pages.

Too Expensive, too Late ... Cancelled!

You don't really want to admit it and often try to hide it, but many projects are not successful. What becomes known about failed projects is only the tip of the iceberg. That means: Project budgets and schedules are severely exceeded, project results are only delivered partially or in poor quality, or projects are cancelled before finalization. The much quoted and periodically released "Chaos Report" of the Standish Group about IT-projects in the USA showed us the following in 1998:

74% of all projects end way above the defined budget or the defined target date or do not deliver the originally defined features or functions.

- 28% of the projects fail and are being cancelled.
- 52% of all IT-projects cost 189% more than originally planned.
- Many projects don't get done even after large investments in time and money.
- Every year, $75 billion are being spent for failed projects in the USA.
- Large projects fail more often.

Projects are complex and every project is different. Taking risks is required for the daily project routine; therefore, every project sets high requirements for the project manager and his team. The results of the recent "Chaos Report" have somewhat improved, but there is still a lot to do. These challenges need to be managed. Whoever has the risks under control sleeps better and won't be taken by surprise because of problems.

The others are to blame!

As the "Chaos Report" of the Standish Group shows, over 74% of the projects fail in some way. What leads to this poor performance? Is it the tools that your project team uses? Is it the high demands? Is it the quality of the data that the project team uses? If you ask the project manager or the team members for the reasons, then you'll receive astonishing answers. You mostly hear complaints about not enough resources, not enough time, and not enough support from senior management or the unreliable suppliers. It's somehow always the fault of others. Is it really like that? Why don't we first look for the problem closer to home? This way, you would probably realize that you didn't have the risks under control!

> **Are the others also always to blame for your project problems?**

Suppressing Risks is our biggest Enemy!

Why do so many projects fail? I always give the same answer to this question: "Projects fail on risks!". Risks, which haven't been taken notice of at all or only a little, cause most of the problems in projects. Maybe the risks haven't been discovered in the risk analysis, which is possible. But let's be honest: Aren't we often endlessly optimistic when it comes to projects – and thereby only see the good sides? Frequently, another important factor is added: the risks are simply being suppressed! I claim that suppressing risks is the biggest enemy for the success of a project. You don't believe me? Then, I have a few questions for you:

- Does your senior management care about the risks in a projects? If yes, is it only superficially or seriously?

- How many projects in your company can present a detailed risk analysis? All of them or only a few?

- How fast is the risk analysis done in your company? In two hours and then never again?

- Are more than ten real risks being discovered during your risk analysis or have only current problems been listed?

Risks are Unpleasant – Suppressing them is Better!

It always amazes me how highly educated senior managers and project managers often ignore the loss potential of risks. What are the reasons for this behavior? The following points show some tendencies:

- Dealing with risks is unpleasant.
- You refuse to believe that a loss potential exists.
- If the possible loss potential were to be acknowledged, then the proposed project would probably not be started.
- You don't want to know or hear about any risks. You already have a lot of other problems.
- Senior management and project managers are optimists by nature: "It's rather unlikely that this risk will materialize."

Would these people react the same way if it were about their own funds and their own savings or would their attitude abruptly change?

You can't make risks disappear that easily because you do not like bad news. To ignore or suppress risks would especially be a very bad tactic.

"Ignoring risks does not make them go away!"

What is the Benefit of Risk Management?

Projects are started based on uncertain information: Uncertain requirements and markets, assumptions, dependencies, and uncertainties in
project execution. Those are base loads, which a project has to carry.
That means every project can turn into a potential failure. Is the use of
risk management really any good to prevent failures or do its cost and
benefit just overrule each other? Is risk management a waste of time? I
can't give you a simple answer to this question because the cost-benefit
ratio essentially depends on the company and project culture. Basically,
risk management, adjusted to project size and the complexity of the project, is worth it a number of times.

Which company is more successful: one that conducts 100 risky projects
or one that has 100 low-risk projects? Risky projects normally have a
much greater profit- and loss potential. The motto is: Exploit the profit
potential and reduce the loss potential. If senior management has the
courage to take risks but can also say NO in an early project stage and
cancels projects with a high risk or minor probability of success, then the
profit potential is accordingly high.

Gartner Group estimates that with an established project risk
management, depending on industry, approximately 20% of the projects
are canceled after the planning-/concept
phase, before the big money is spent in the
execution phase. If 70 of the 100 high-risk
projects survive after the planning/concept
phase and continue to be subject to consistent risk management, then
success isn't far away.

> **Whoever doesn't take a risk, will definitely stagnate!**

Risk has a direct relation to profit. Simply put: the more risks a company is willing to take with its projects, the higher the possible benefits
can be – but only if you have the risks under control with consistently
applied risk management on a project and company level. Whoever
doesn't take any risks, will definitely stagnate!

A Matter of Conviction

Do you know what you will face if you don't properly deal with your
project risks? Often, you're lucky and it doesn't happen much. However,
the hammer will eventually strike and you will be confronted with prob-

lems and disasters, which you were afraid to imagine in your thoughts. Is it a problem for you...

- ... if the project takes much longer?
- ... if the project costs much more?
- ... if the project doesn't achieve the required performance?
- ... if customer satisfaction massively drops?
- ... if the reputation of your company is ruined?
- ... if you don't have a job anymore?

If none of these represent a problem for you, then you can refrain from risk management!

Risk Management Standards and Guidelines for Projects

For project risk management, there are some relevant standards and guidelines. The most important is the IEC 62198:2001. It was taken over unchanged into the DIN IEC 62198:2002-09. This standard gives a general introduction into project risk management and provides some guidance. In the list below, you will find an overview of the most important risk management standards, which concern projects:

- DIN IEC 62198:2002-09: "Project Risk Management - Application guidelines"
- Association for Project Management: "Project Risk Analysis & Management Guide" (PRAM Guide), 2nd Edition 2004
- British Standard BS6079-3:2000: "Project Management – Guide to the management of business-related project risk"
- Institution of Civil Engineers (ICE) and the Actuarial Professional: "Risk Analysis and Management for Projects (RAMP) 2002"
- Project Management Institute: "A Guide to the Project Management Body of Knowledge (PMBOK® Guide)", Fifth Edition 2013 – Chapter 11 „Project Risk Management".
- US Department of Defense: "Risk Management Guide for DoD Acquisition", Sixth Edition, August 2006

There are many other standards and guidelines in which risk management in projects is a topic. These include: COBIT, BOOT-STRAP, CMMI, DriveSPI. In these guidelines, however, other elements, e.g. quality management or IT-relevant topics, have a much larger coverage. In my opinion, one of the most important standard is the PMBOK® Guide of the PMI, Chapter 11 "Project Risk Management".

The Risk Management Process

● ●

Risk Management is a Process

Risk management is a process that, regardless of the project duration and the complexity of the project, will not just be executed once but again and again. In the following figure on the next page, you will see the activities of the risk management process, which is based on the PMBOK® Guide of the PMI. These activities form a closed loop. Risk management planning lies outside of the loop because it is created at the beginning of the project and only adjusted as needed. Now and then, it is taken by the hand again, for example, if questions arise about risk management in the project or when new employees entering the project need to be trained.

The most important step of the risk management process is risk identification because only risks that are identified can be analyzed and treated with appropriate actions. Therefore, risk identification takes up most of the space in this book. The continuous communication is a central element of the risk management process and is constantly used. That is why communication doesn't lie on the closed loop but rather in the center. If risks are being communicated and remain a constant topic, then this automatically contributes to their reduction.

> **The most important step in the risk management process is the risk identification**

Figure 2: The Risk Management Process

Risk Management Planning: Define how risk management will be done on the project, who will be involved with which responsibilities, which processes will be used, and which activities will be conducted.

Risk Identification: Identify risks and opportunities that affect the project or individual work packages/activities. Create a detailed list of all risks.

Risk Analysis (qualitative/quantitative): Analyze the collected risks and determine which risks are further tracked. For these risks, determine impact (positive/negative) and probability qualitatively. Depending on project size, or company internal rules, the risks are also quantitatively evaluated and then prioritized.

Risk Response Planning: Define actions for each risk, to reduce the probability and/or impact of risks or to increase probability and/or impact of opportunities. The actions are then implemented.

Monitoring and Control: Implement risk response plans. Monitor and assess initiated actions and risks periodically. If necessary, adjust actions or define new actions. Perform risk reviews.

Communication: Communicate periodically, project-internally and externally, existing and new risks and other risk management activities.

Risk Management is more than just Risk Analysis!

Risk management is frequently put on a level with risk analysis. That's not true, though! Analysis is only the exact examination of the specifics. Before risks can be analyzed, you have to identify them. The risks are being more closely examined in the process step "Analysis" to be able to understand them better. Afterward, probability and impact can be evaluated. Then, planning responses, monitoring and control will follow, and last but not least, the communication of risks and actions mustn't be forgotten.

A Continuous Process – No One-Off!

In project execution, the following is often observed: Risk management only begins when risks are evident, which normally means that they have materialized or are foreseeable. Risk management in such cases is only used as crisis management, when it is too late.

"We have carried out risk management after the kick-off. The topic is now done for us. Now we can dedicate our precious time to the actual project activities again." Unfortunately, this statement is herard very often. Have you done your duties at the beginning of the project, if you've identified and assessed the risks and defined and initiated actions? What do you think? I hope you are saying "No, that's not enough!"

The above-mentioned examples show that risk management in projects ...

- has to begin early on and
- is to be repeated periodically/permanently

The fact that risk potentials already exist in its roots before or at the beginning of projects and are recognizable shows the necessity to start early on with risk management. Risks are waiting to unexpectedly surprise you during project execution and cause as much damage as possible. Risk management therefore has to begin before project start and is no one-time activity but rather a permanent duty, which accompanies the project team from project start through to the end of the project. The risk management process will not only be

> **Risk management is no one-off but rather a permanent duty!**

passed through once but again and again, depending on project duration and the complexity of the project. More on the subject of risk management before project start can be found on page 26.

Risk Management Definitions

There are many definitions for project risk management. The following is my view the best and leans on the PMBOK® Guide:

Project Risk Management is a systematic, proactive process, which identifies, analyzes and responses to risk. The objectives of Project Risk Management are to increase the probability and impact of positive events and decrease the probability and impact of negative events in the project.

Definition of Project Risk

There are also many definitions for project risk. One of the best is that of the PMBOK® Guide. This defines project risk as follows:

Project Risk is an uncertain future event or condition that, if it occurs, has a negative or positive effect on at least on project objective. Objectives can include scope, schedule, cost and quality. A risk may have one or more causes and, if it occurs, it may have one or more impacts.

A risk is an **uncertainty**, which threatens the **project goals**. This uncertainty is a potential future problem (or opportunity), which hasn't occurred yet but will occur with a certain probability.

The term project risk describes, according to the following formula, a possible damage (or benefit) which occurs when **no** measures are taken.

$$\text{Project Risk} = \text{Probability} \times \text{Impact}$$

The Probability

The first factor which determines project risk is the probability. It expresses the possibility that an event (risk) occurs. It reaches from 0% (will not occur) up to 100% (will definitely occur).

The possibility is considered a predictable factor in mathematics. In practice, you usually abstain from complicated calculations and subjectively estimate the probability. Your project team and experts are a good help thereby.

The Impact

The second factor, which determines the size of the project risk, is the impact. It describes the possible damage (or benefit) when the risk actually occurs. The term "damage" can be broadly defined. It could, for example, mean the destruction of material or buildings, damage due to failure to meet the deadlines or poor work performance. The benefit, for example, shows itself in unexpected price cuts of the contractor, new unexpected technological insights, or change in laws, which serve the project goals.

The damage or the benefit always has an effect in project execution on the three competing sizes in project management: cost, time, quality/performance.

Even though one of these three factors is affected, the damage or the benefit usually has a monetary impact in the end. For example, poor quality has long-term consequences because developed products have to be recalled after project closure, accidents occur or customers back out. A delay in the deadline has to be financially reimbursed very often or due to poor work performance; the project needs more resources to be able to get done on schedule.

The Levels of Risk Management

"Precaution is better than healing." This statement is one you probably know from healthcare. It also applies to projects. Unfortunately, precaution isn't always the most used strategy regarding projects. It mostly stays at waiting and accepting risks, in the hope that nothing happens. The following list shows the levels of how to react to risks: from eliminating the root cause up to putting out the fire.

1. **Eliminate root causes:** Identify and eliminate conditions that make it possible for risks to even exist.

2. **Eliminate risks:** Systematically identify and analyze risks as well as implement preventive actions so that the risks have no chance of becoming a problem.

3. **Reduce risks:** Plan measures to reduce the probability and impact of a risk.

4. **React on risk event:** Don't reduce identified risks but rather react fast with an emergency plan when they occur.

5. **Crisis management:** Put out the fire. Treat not identified risks which have occurred and have become a problem.

On which level do you find yourself most of the time? As a project manager, you're probably confronted with all levels because the everyday project life is apparently unpredictable – and you can't find all risks for sure. You can, however, save yourself a lot of money, worries and troubles if you deal with risks early on and continually manage these. That is why your preferred main activities are located on level 1 through 3. Money invested on these levels, is well spent. If you follow these levels, then you won't become a fireman who is constantly putting out the fire at different places!

"..... good managers manage risks, bad managers manage problems."

Risk Management before Project Start

The earlier you deal with risks in projects, the better! A lack of many project risk management processes is that they begin after project start. It is crucial to deal with risks already during the acquisition or the preparation phase of the project. This "strategic risk management" is basically concerned with the following questions:

- What is the risk, if we carry out the project?
- What is the risk, if we don't carry out the project or refrain from a quotation submittal?

The answers to these questions, including further criteria, help with the "go" or "no-go" decision and with the prioritization of the projects in the project portfolio.

The Initialization Phase of Internal Projects

The initialization phase of internal projects lasts through the preparation phase of the project from the first idea up to the decision of the executive management to actually start the project.

A decision-making basis for the prioritization of the project is required for the annual project budgeting in the late summer or the continuous project portfolio planning. The basis for decision is mostly a project proposal and/or a business case, in which the main points of the project are described. The most important contents are: the relationship of the project to the strategy/medium-term goals of the company, the cost-benefit calculation and the risks of the project. The risk analysis is thereby a substantial basis for decision-making for a "go" or "no-go" decision. In this project status, it usually consists of a list with different questions e.g. about project size in Dollar, number of project team members, complexity of the technical solution etc. Each question will be assessed and rated. The evaluated risk list gives the risk classification figure for the project, which then is incorporated into the decision-making process.

The initialization phase of external projects

For projects with external clients, the initialization phase of the project consists of two steps:

1. From the first customer contact to the decision, to make a quotation (pre-bid phase)
2. From the decision to develop an offer, to the completion of a contract (bid phase)

A basis for decision-making is created in the pre-bid phase on which it will be decided whether or not to create a quotation. Besides technical feasibility, strategic and economic aspects, the risk analysis is the most important element for the decision-making.

The bid phase reaches from the decision to develop a quotation, deliver it and negotiate it up to the decision to accept the order. Up to the definite quotation submittal, the risk analysis should furthermore clarify in detail if an offer contains special risks in regards to price, deadline and formulated work or services offered. When the quotation is completed, a detailed overview about all risks should be available and corresponding actions should be defined or be contained in the quotation.

With a systematic contract review in the bid phase, you will avoid many risks.

Practice shows, that most of the risks for the further project execution are defined because of shortcomings in the initialization phase. On one hand, this is because of a lack of clarification effort or lack of knowledge of contractual basics. Typical deficiencies in this phase, for example, are:

- vague, interpretable contract formulations
- pending points, which still have to be resolved in the later project phases
- not clearly defined project scope or requirements

Deficiencies in this phase can, for the greater part, be avoided through a systematic contract review. I recommend, especially for large orders, to bring in the internal legal department or other experts specialized in contract law of the respective branch and to conduct a detailed contract review. This risk reducing measure always pays off.

Risk Management Planning

● ●

Only What is Planned, Will Also be Carried Out

The risk management plan describes how risk management is structured in your project and how it is carried out. It is an excellent tool to organize the entire risk management of the project. If your organization has specific guidelines for risk management, it is worthwhile to break these down to your project and to define it more specifically.

The most important result in this step is the risk management plan, which according to PMBOK®, is a component of the project management plan. A second important point is the training of the project participants in risk management.

In risk management planning, you should note that the risk management activities need to be tailored to the project concerned, which means, they should be appropriate in terms of:

- the size, complexity and duration of the project
- the already known risks of the project
- the importance of the project for the organisation

For smaller, simpler projects, a separate risk management plan is not necessary. The project risk management procedure can, in this case, be described directly in the project management plan. The risk management plan is created by the project manager, often with the assistance of the project team, the project risk officers and maybe further necessary stakeholders.

The Risk Management Plan

The extent of the risk management plan is highly dependent on the size, complexity and duration of the project as well as on the already existing guidelines in the company. However, you should at least define the following chapters in the risk management plan, which the PMBOK® Guide of the PMI also describes:

- **Methodology:** Define procedure, data source and tools, which are used for the execution of risk management.
- **Roles and Responsibilities:** Define roles and responsibilities for risk management in the project as well as the persons involved by name.
- **Budget:** Define resources and estimated costs for risk management. These are a part of the project cost planning.
- **Schedule:** Define how often you will carry out which risk management activities during the project life cycle and define these in the project plan.
- **Risk Categories:** Define a structure with risk categories and subcategories which will help you to identify risks efficiently and improve the quality in the risk management process.
- **Definition of Probability and Impact:** Define the terms and scales which you use for the probability and impact in the qualitative risk analysis. Make sure that the risk assessments are comparable between projects.
- **Risk Matrix:** Decide in which position in the risk matrix, actions will be defined for risks.
- **Reporting:** Define the content and the form of the risk management report to be applied. Define how the results of the risk management process will be documented.
- **Monitoring:** Define how to monitor risks and measures and whether risk management of the project will be reviewed or audited. Describe whether lessons learned for future projects will be documented.
- **Communication:** Define to whom, what, in which intervals will be reported and who has access to risk information.

Roles and Responsibilities

In order for risk management to be carried out effectively, there are several responsible people in the project.

Project Manager: He is responsible that risk management in the project will be established, actively carried out and lived. He carries overall responsibility for risk management and reports to the project sponsor and the steering committee.

Project Risk Officer: He possesses in-depth risk management know-how and supports the project manager and the sub-project managers and is co-responsible that risk management will be established, carried out and controlled according to company guidelines. For smaller projects, the project manager, or a different person from the PMO, takes over the role of the project risk officer.

Sub-project Manager: He is responsible that risk management will be established in the sub-project, actively carried out and lived.

Project Team Member (Risk Owner): He is responsible for the risks of his work packages. He reports newly found risks immediately, monitors his risks continually and carries out the delegated actions.

Do We Need a Risk Board?

Special risk boards, bodies or committees are often not necessary and often lead to an over-organization. For very large projects of over 20 million Dollars, however, such bodies can be useful. More important is that risks and risk management are a constant agenda item during periodic project team meetings. For further risk activities, workshops or working groups are ideal.

Risk Management Training for Everyone!

Many project team members don't know much about risks – unfortunately, this frequently also applies to many project managers. In addition to risk management planning, it is therefore useful to carry out a quick training for all project team members. This training only requires 1-2 hours. It gives the project team members a basic knowledge of project risk manage-

Risk management training for project team members is always worth it!

ment and provides them their duties, responsibility and authority in risk management during the project process. This training should be carried out by a specialist who knows the company-specific risk management guidelines and is also fit in project risk management. For example, this can be a risk officer or a specialist from the PMO.

▶ Contact experienced project managers and ask them how they set-up their risk management.

▶ Keep your risk management organisation simple.

▶ Define the roles and responsibilities of risk management in your project and talk about these.

▶ Carry out a short risk management training for all project team members.

Risk Identification

5

● ●

The Most Important Step in Risk Management

In risk identification, you are looking for all imaginable risks and opportunities that could arise during the project. But the identified risks and opportunities will not yet have been evaluated. Risk identification is the most important step in the risk management process because risks which aren't found cannot be dealt with. Recognized and accepted risks are already half-controlled risks!

> *Try to find possible problems before they arise,*
> *because...anything that can go wrong, will go wrong.*
> *(Murphy's Risk Management Law)*

Eduard Murphy's worldly wisdom of human failure, or rather about the sources of error in complex systems, very vividly shows what could head our way. "Anything that can go wrong, will go wrong – it's only a matter of time." If you approach risk identification with this attitude, then you're already well-equipped. This is one side of risk identification, the negative view. It will be more difficult if you have to switch to the positive side according to the motto: "Opportunities present themselves everywhere – you only have to use them!" The "positive risks", which means to find opportunities, are also a component of risk identification. Unfortunately, this part is often forgotten or neglected.

Main goals of risk identification are:

- Create a list as long as possible with risks and opportunities, which could affect the project as a whole, single work packages or activities.

- Make sure that all risk categories are considered upon risk identification.

- Make sure that all risks are understood.

Identifying risks is not a job for the project manager behind closed doors but rather teamwork! The project manager, the project team, the project sponsor, specialists and every person involved in the project will thereby **Identifying risks is teamwork** be working on this. During risk identification all found risks will be documented. This includes a detailed description of the risk, its cause and effect.

It is an open secret: Risks, which are identified, occur less likely. This is because they have changed from the state of the "unknown unknown" to the "known unknown". And as soon as risks are identified, documented, and talked about, and the more you deal with them, the less dangerous they are. Risk identification therefore already lowers the overall risk of the project. Risk identification is the most important step in risk management!

If you keep the following experiences from Eduard Murphy in mind, which are to be observed daily, then you will also probably notice risks more in the future:

- If anything can go wrong, it will (Main rule).

- If anything can go wrong in different ways, then it will always go wrong in the way in which it causes the most damage.

- If you've ruled out all possibilities of things that could go wrong, a new possibility will open up immediately.

- The likeliness that a certain event occurs is inversely proportional to its desirability.

- Sooner or later, the worst possible linkage of circumstances will occur.

Describe Risks Clearly

Describing risks isn't that easy. In practice you'll see a lot of inaccurate and far too little described risks which do not reveal anything, which nobody understands exactly what is meant by that. The more exact and specific you describe your risks, the more specific you can later define the actions hereof and the more effective your risk management is.

Only if you formulate the risks systematically and thoroughly, you can make sure:

- that everyone understands which specific risk it's about
- that the identified risk will be accepted as relevant
- that the right actions are taken

The "Cause – Risk – Impact" Format

Risks are very often mistaken with facts or current problems but also often with causes from which risks arise. To be able to clearly and specifi-

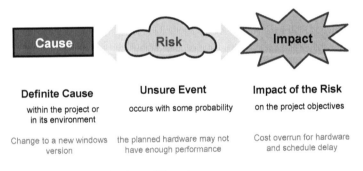

Definite Cause	Unsure Event	Impact of the Risk
within the project or in its environment	occurs with some probability	on the project objectives
Change to a new windows version	the planned hardware may not have enough performance	Cost overrun for hardware and schedule delay

Figure 3: „Cause - Risk – Impact" Format

cally define risks, you should use the "Cause – Risk – Impact" format. With this format, you have to make more of an effort upon defining the risks. However, this helps you deal with risks more intensively and to clearly separate risks from causes and impacts. In order for you to describe risks unmistakably, you should use the following three-piece sentence format:

Because of the <**cause**>, the <**risk**> can arise, which will then have this <**impact**>.

This structure of a sentence helps you focus on the actual risks. It can also be used to "generate" risks if you're assuming the one or the other end (from causes or impacts so to speak).

What are Causes?

Causes are definitive events/facts or a number of circumstances which already exist in the project or its environment, or whose existence is secure in the future and give rise to uncertainty. That means that these causes can trigger risks. Causes are not uncertain and that is why they are not to be confused with risks.

Examples for causes are the requirements to carry out the project in a developing nation, the necessity to use a non-approved technique, or the absence of qualified personnel.

What are Risks?

Risks are uncertainties that can affect the project goals either negatively or positively (opportunities) if they occur. Examples for that are the possibility that the planned efficiency goals may not be able to be adhered to, customer expectations will be misunderstood, or that storms can delay the assembly. These uncertainties can be treated actively with actions.

What are Impacts?

Impacts are unplanned negative or positive deviations of the project goals which can arise as a result of occurred risks. Examples for that are: Less insurance policies than planned are sold or the machine is heavier than specified. Impacts are possible events or potential deviations that only arise when risks occur.

Look for the Root Causes and Go into Detail

Watch out! A lot of the identified risks are often not the real risk, but rather impacts. The real risks not uncommonly lie deeper. Therefore you should attempt to search for the root causes to be certain to treat the right risks. You'll get to the bottom of the causes with multiple "Why questions".

Consider the Time of Occurrence

Certain risks can only arise at a certain time or in a certain period. Therefore you should also ask the following question during risk identification in a second step: "When can risks possibly occur?" With this question, it will be easier for you to determine a possible time of occurrence for the risk. The answer then helps you shape the response planning in a way that you can initiate effective actions in time. There are five possibilities for the time of occurrence of a risk:

- Anytime
- At a certain point in time
- No later than a certain point in time
- Only at a certain point in time
- In a certain period of time

Identifying Opportunities

When you look for risks, you should also always have the opportunities in focus. But why do you see opportunities in risk registers so rarely? This has a simple reason: It's not that easy identifying opportunities! It's in the nature of humans to rather deal with negative things but this is also often in our negative adjusted mentality. You're probably going to agree with me when I say that it's easier to identify potential traps and problems than hidden advantages and good opportunities. That is why we have to take more time and

Identified opportunities are "Added Value" for the project.

make more of an effort to identify opportunities. It is certainly not easy reversing itself and presenting events and positive opportunities of influence that support and promote the achievement of the project goal. Try it – it's worth it!

▶ Describe the risks in detail and don't settle for general, unspecific statements too quickly.

▶ Always describe the risks in "Cause/Risk/Impact" format.

▶ Get to the bottom of the causes to find the real risks.

▶ Also try to find opportunities – even if it's not that easy.

From Risk Management to Problem Management

A project without problems is as little as a life without death, because projects per definition are already risky and problematic. Project management offers effective tools to approach these obstacles with risk and problem management. However, the difference between problems and risks is unclear to many project managers. Being able to recognize this difference is very crucial for effective project risk management.

Talking about risks is not well-received … you already have enough problems!

If nobody speaks about risks during project execution then you'll probably struggle with problems many times. These problems have with certainty risen from risks, that no one paid attention to in the past.

Risk or Problem?

The answer to this question has a wide influence on your further activities. Is it a risk or a problem? As you may remember: a risk is an uncertainty. If this uncertainty becomes a certainty, that means if the risks materialize, then you have a problem. This practically always has an effect on costs, time, quality/performance of the project.

Risk = Uncertainty	→ can possibly materialize
Problem = Fact, Security	→ exists or materialized

"A lack of resources" or an "insufficient budget" aren't examples of a risk. This is also true for the fact that there is "too little time to complete the project". If it's known that the provided amount of time is insufficient to complete the project, then it's not an uncertainty, but a fact, or respectively a problem for you. Such facts need to be dealt with by you and therefore taken into account when it comes to project planning. But there is something that you have to pay attention to: Although these statements don't portray a risk, they can be the cause of future risks.

> It's crucial to know the difference between a risk and a problem.

Is a risk with an 80% probability still a risk? A percentage of 80% means that something is very likely to occur. Therefore it's actually not an uncertainty, but a certainty, which means a fact or an actual problem. Such risks should be provided directly to problem management. The following figure shows the difference between a problem and a risk from another side.

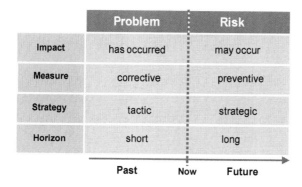

	Problem	Risk
Impact	has occurred	may occur
Measure	corrective	preventive
Strategy	tactic	strategic
Horizon	short	long

Past   Now   Future

Figure 4: The Difference Between Risk and Problem

The Knowns and the Unknowns

The knowledge of uncertain circumstances can have a different magnitude during the course of a project. You can differentiate between the following three uncertainty levels:

- "The known knowns"
- "The known unknowns"
- "The unknown unknowns"

This word play might be a bit confusing for you at the beginning. In the following lines, you'll find a logic explanation for it. The "knowns" are knowledge that the project already possesses. In connection with risk management, these knowns are often confused with risks, although they're actual known problems. This is a task for problem management.

The following figure shows the relation between the degree of knowledge about risks, the respective approach, and the utilized management method.

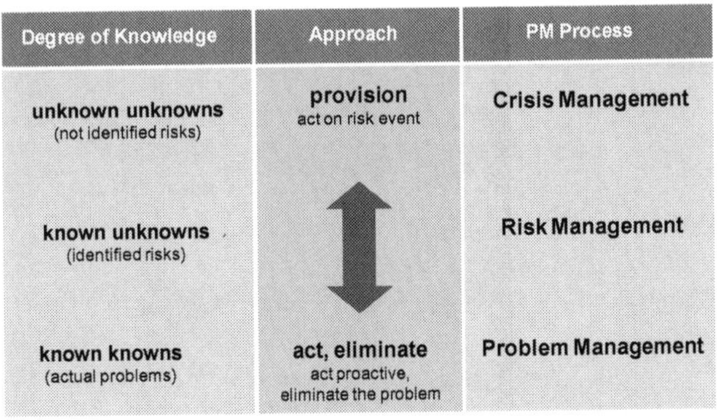

Degree of Knowledge	Approach	PM Process
unknown unknowns (not identified risks)	**provision** act on risk event	**Crisis Management**
known unknowns (identified risks)		**Risk Management**
known knowns (actual problems)	**act, eliminate** act proactive, eliminate the problem	**Problem Management**

Figure 5: The Right PM Process for Knowns and Unknonws

The "known unknowns" are risks that were identified in the risk analysis. If it's useful, you should take actions against these known uncertainties, which can have a positive or negative impact on the project – either to prevent damage or to be able to take advantage of possible opportunities.

The "unknown unknowns" are risks that couldn't be identified in the risk analysis, but exist. The potential danger exists, but you aren't aware of it. Sometime during project execution, you might get confronted with the impact of such a risk without a forewarning. Then the crisis management ability of the project manager is in demand.

> *"Powerful project managers don't solve problems, they get rid of them."*

Take this saying to heart. Don't try to avoid definitive problems and invest enough time into risk management! Only this way "unknown unknowns" can turn into known risks that you can manage.

Methods of Risk Identification

There are different methods that you can use to identify risks, which range from simple to costly. Unfortunately, often only one method is used for the identification of risks, which is the checklist. The advantage of checklists is obvious: One doesn't have to think much during work, but the yield of relevant risks is rather low. Only with different methods and sources of information you'll have a chance to discover the largest possible amount of relevant risks. Every method used provides a different viewpoint towards the project. You can use valuable knowledge with the different participants. The possible methods of identification range from rather formulaic methods like checklists to intuitive methods like brainstorming.

Proven methods for the identification of risks:

- Document analysis and historic records
- Evaluation of risk registers and lessons learned from similar projects
- Brainstorming with the project team and experts
- Interviews with domain experts and other project managers
- Brainwriting, i.e. Method 635
- Delphi Method
- Risk checklists with risk categories and risks

You can find out more about the methods on the following pages. With this knowledge, you can design a more effective risk identification approach for your project.

Document Analysis and Historic Records

Analyze all important project documents and records for project risks. These are for example:

- Statement of work, project requirements, functional specifications
- Tender documents
- Contracts with the customer or suppliers
- Specifications

- Drawings
- Lists with assumptions and restrictions
- Work breakdown structure (WBS), Work package descriptions

Are some documents missing in your project? Do you have a project charter with clear goals? Do you have a work breakdown structure? Are the contracts with the customers and suppliers in compliance with the local laws? Was there a contract review? Are descriptions available for all work packages? Are all deliverables clearly documented? If important documents are missing you'll have additional risks in your project!

Pay attention to possible risks of legal regulations that might apply to your project, such as:

- Customs regulations
- Standards
- Country specific laws
- Environmental regulations

Problems in projects have the tendency to repeat themselves in other projects in similar ways. Due to this, you can find possible risks upon the consultation of risk registers and lessons learned from completed projects.

Brainstorming

Brainstorming is one of the best and most effective methods for the identification of risks. You most likely already work with brainstorming. This method is widely used and successfully applied in many companies. If you don't know brainstorming yet, then you'll receive a short introduction here.

Brainstorming is a creative method to find ideas in a group. This method is really helpful for identifying risks, but also works for

> **Brainstorming is one of the best methods for the identification of risks.**

other project management tasks. A fundamental characteristic of brainstorming is the associative, non-interpreted collection of a large amount of spontaneous answers to a specific question – in this case, project risks.

The advantage of brainstorming in a group is the mutual stimulus of the participants, while the disadvantage is the possible focus on a single aspect. After the collection of ideas through brainstorming, the discovered risks have to be sorted and roughly evaluated.

Do you think that you already know everything about brainstorming? There might be a few points that you haven't considered yet. The following procedural description might improve the way you conduct brainstorming.

The identification of risks with brainstorming:

1. Decide who is supposed to participate in the brainstorming session. You can conduct multiple sessions with different groups, e.g. with the project team, stakeholders, end users or developers.

2. Find two writers because it's difficult to record every quickly rising thought with just one person. With a second person, you can make sure that all ideas are recorded fully and correctly.

3. Instruct the writers to write the risks on a flipchart or even better on pinboard cards in sufficiently large font.

4. Instruct the participants of the brainstorming: "The goal of this session is to collect a large amount of risks in the shortest possible amount of time. Don't judge the ideas when they come to your mind; just let your thoughts flow freely. The risks can be utopian, too. Don't judge the ideas of other participants, either."

5. Ask about the risks for the whole project.

6. Ask about risks of specific areas of interest or regarding specific project phases.

7. Group the risks by similar categories within the session or shortly thereafter and sort out duplicate risks.

8. Write down who declared the risk. If something is unclear or if you need to be able to understand the risks more clearly, you can ask the specific participant. The risk should be described clearly and understood by everyone involved.

9. Describe the risks in a "Cause – Risk – Impact" Format.

How to get the most out of your brainstorming session

- Don't rate any answers. A rating would hamper the flow of ideas, slow down the progress and demotivate the participants.

- Find a way to get everyone to participate in a session, e.g. through using pinboard cards or asking the people you want to participate directly, especially the introverted ones.

- Try to let everyone provide his ideas and make sure nobody is talking too extensively.

- Write the brainstorming rules on a flipchart and remind people about them when appropriate.

- Make the list of risks as long as possible. Remember: Quantity before quality.

- The more unusual the ideas, the better. Let your fantasies flow freely.

- The improvement or extension of already mentioned ideas is allowed.

- Ratings and critiques are not allowed, neither verbally or via body language e.g. shaking one's head or sniffing at something.

- If no additional risks are mentioned after a couple of minutes, the risk catalog with the risk categories or specific questions by the moderator might provide new stimuli.

- Make some short breaks during the brainstorming session, in which participants can reflect and write down more ideas for themself.

- Define an additional, anonymous reporting channel, where anyone can report the "craziest" risks, or which they do not want to say in "public".

Brainstorming is the best method to identify risks in my opinion. It shouldn't, however, be the only method in use.

Expert Interviews

Expert interviews can be used for most steps of project risk management. Experts, customers, senior management or specialist departments in the company, like legal departments, can often aid in identifying risks. The benefit of such interviews is often underestimated.

Expert interviews are best conducted by you personally. If there are time, distance or availability issues, these can also be done via phone or e-mail. Interviews aren't informal chats; they have to be planned in advance, organized and monitored to be effective.

You shouldn't go alone to expert interviews, if possible. If you're alone, you're likely to miss a lot of verbal and non-verbal information of the expert. The role of the companion should be clarified in advance to avoid disruptions and ambiguities. Normally one person asks the questions and the second person writes down the answers.

Advantages of Expert Interviews:

- New risks from specific specialist fields are uncovered that would be impossible to uncover through the use of other sources.

- You will receive specific information about the probability of occurrence, impact, possible actions and emergency plans.

- You receive sustained support for the project as the relevant stakeholders are informed now and keep things in mind subconsciously.

How you can get the most of your expert interview:

- Don't go to expert interviews alone. If you're alone, you'll miss a great deal of the verbal and non-verbal information from the expert.

- Don't be satisfied with the first answer right away. Dig deeper and look for more than the things that have been said already. You should avoid turning it into an interrogation though.

- After the interview discuss the answers and your interpretation of them with your assistant. You should also invite other project members to join the discussion.

Brainwriting

Brainwriting is a modification of brainstorming and stands for a number of methods and variants. Examples for brainwriting methods are:

- Method 635
- Map Technique
- Brainwriting Pool
- Collective Notebook

Brainwriting is applied like brainstorming, to identify risks and to find ideas about possible actions. Brainwriting can be used as a group technique or for a single person. The rules of brainwriting are a bit more complex than those for brainstorming. A mutual stimulation is mostly reached through speaking and listing when it comes to brainstorming, while for brainwriting every participant is writing down their associations by themselves on a large paper sheet.

Through writing, it's possible to have multiple independent chains of association at the same time, while brainstorming poses the risk that only the loudest person in the room will dominate the train of thought. The disadvantage of writing is the fact that not everybody can perceive everything at the same time.

The particular aspect of brainwriting in comparison to brainstorming is the fact that every participant can collect his ideas by himself, without rush and write them down. This brings an advantage to introverted participants that can't assert themselves verbally, or choose not to do so. It allows both extroverted and introverted individuals to pass on their ideas. For a larger group of participants, it's advisable that the paper is not attached to a moderation board, but to a large table, which allows multiple persons to write at the same time

The Rules of Brainwriting

Just as with brainstorming, a particular importance is given to reduction of all factors that could limit the production of new ideas. At the same time, special attention should be given to all factors that enhance the process of combination. The participants should produce ideas without any limitation and combine ideas with each other. Brainwriting is separated into two phases: The first phase is about developing as many ideas and associations as possible. In this phase the assessment of other ideas as well as own ideas, are not allowed, as this could lead to an inner censorship of the participants, which would make the discovery of new ideas harder. In the second phase, the results undergo a thorough criticism and the best ideas are pulled out.

Advantages of Brainwriting

- Easy to handle
- Produces lots of new ideas in a relatively short amount of time
- Ideas aren't discussed to death
- You can get inspired by the ideas of other participants

Method 635 is best suited for practicing brainwriting in a group. You can find further information at: http://en.wikipedia.org/wiki/6-3-5_Brainwriting

Risk Categories

Risk categories help with a systematic identification of risks and add to the effectiveness and quality of risk identification. Risk categories can be very different, depending on the industry or the type of project.

In the following figure, you can see the risk categories with subcategories for risks that are typical for projects in the insurance industry. Possible risks are then added to the subcategories. A risk checklist can be created as a result of this exercise that gives indications on new risks and opportunities.

> **Risk categories help to find new risks after the brainstorming.**

The illustration with risk categories and subcategories offers a good assistance for the identification of risks. The first activity for the identification of risks, however, should always be a brainstorming with the project team and a questioning of experts.

At the end of the brainstorming, when the flow of ideas has stopped, you'll be able to uncover undiscovered risks again with the risk categories and checklists. This also makes sure that you haven't forgotten any risk categories or subcategories. On the following page you'll get to know the main categories.

Project Management Risks	Leading and Organizational Risks	Technical Risk	Commercial Risks	Project Environme Risks
Project Scope	Leadership Responsibility	Requirements Specification	Contracts	Politics, Law
Complexity	Support, Commitment	Technology, Hardware, Software	Suppliers	Competitors
Schedule	Project Organization Resources	Interface, Complexity	Financials	Customers
Cost	Impact on Company Organization	Performance, Reliability	Profitability	Stakeholders
Communication	Change Management	Quality		

Figure 6: Typical Project Risk Categories in the Insurance Industry

Project Management Risks

Project management risks are risks that arise from the size and complexity of the project that have a direct influence on the management of the project. They are also risks that emerge from the act of managing the project and include planning, monitoring and control of the project, as well as the technical guidance of the project team and communication. Project management risks are mainly a result of a lack of experience of the project manager. The risks are an over- or underestimation of the effort and complexity, errors in project planning and budgeting as well as insufficient project controlling and inappropriate communication.

Leading and Organizational Risks

Leadership and organizational risks are exclusively risks that arise in the conjunction with persons or groups of persons. Risks develop when the leadership abilities of the project manager are insufficient and he doesn't assume his responsibility or is unable to assume it. When the support or commitment of the senior management or other important positions is lacking, the risk of a failure or termination of the project is big. Every project has an impact on persons; risks arise when these persons aren't involved in the project and opportunity management is neglected. Sociocultural risks take place for projects in foreign countries when project teams work in foreign countries or when the customer has a different cultural background. Additionally other risks in relation to traditions, moral concepts, culture and nationality can arise during the realization of the project.

Technical Risks

Technical risks aren't just technical uncertainties when it comes to the development and production of products, but also the risks that might occur during the usage of the finished product after the completion of the project. Innovative projects, especially, can have big risks attached to them when it comes to the technical specifications, producibility, verifiability and specific functions of the product.

The technical risks are usually a result of the complexity and novelty of applicable techniques and systems. Those risks can express themselves in a reduced performance, a lowered range of function, lower quality or total uselessness of the product in the worst case scenario. I'm particularly thinking of security risks.

Commercial Risks

Commercial risks encompass uncertainties in the economic area of the project, which means financing, profitability and economic relations with suppliers. The main areas of risk are uncertainties in the profitability calculation, imprecise and interpretable contracts with customers and suppliers as well, as a dependence on suppliers and their services.

Project Environment Risks

The project environment often expresses itself in the form of framework conditions and restrictions that the project is exposed to. This includes political risks in one's own country, but especially in foreign countries for cross-border projects, as for example: import restrictions, tax disadvantages, the danger of being disowned or intransparent legal requirements.

Competitors, which develop similar products and go to market more quickly, might endanger the project, as well as competitors enjoying other advantages. The customer/market as the consumer of the product is also often intransparent and thus often a risk. Stakeholder requirements could lead to sudden unexpected problems. This is a large risk, especially if stakeholders aren't sufficiently involved in the project.

Risk Checklists

Risk checklists for risk identification are used in many companies. The risk checklist is not a creative technique, but if it's used in the right way, it can have a good benefit when it comes to identifying risks. Risk checklists are normally based on the experience that has been collected in previous projects and compiled later on. Checklists have the advantage that they allow you to do a risk analysis relatively fast and easily. That way you're able to get an overview of the project risk in a relatively short amount of time. It makes sense to derive the risk checklist from risk categories. The risk categories get converted into chapters in the risk checklist and the subcategories turn into subchapters.

The "Problem" with Checklists

Checklists can have a big advantage when it comes to the identification of risks, but this is only the case if they're used correctly. You can get quick results with checklists and an overview of the risk of the project. You get led by it and you don't have to think too much. Checklists can have big disadvantages, though, if they're used in the wrong way:

- They provide a false sense of security that all risks have been uncovered.
- It's difficult to think beyond the checklist while filling it out.
- They aren't identifying risks by activity or work package.
- They don't provide enough information about the risks, their causes and the impact.
- They don't give their user the chance to add risks that aren't on the checklist yet.
- They aren't project specific.
- They don't help with the process of rating, qualifying and quantifying risks.

If all resources like brainstorming, expert interviews, etc. have been used and you think that all risks have been found, then a checklist can be a good tool for the project team as the last method in use. They might uncover risks that you might have forgotten otherwise. In my experience, a risk checklist can uncover up to 30% more potential risks at the end.

A mistake that is often made during risk identification, is to forget about risk categories. Can you imagine the consequences if the risk categories, contractual risks and cultural risks are forgotten for an investment project in India? Just have a look at recently finished projects – which risks were unidentified?

▶ Use a combination of methods for identifying risks. You'll be able to find more risks this way.

▶ Define an anonymous reporting channel that allows team members and stakeholders to report "sensible" risks at any time. Not everybody wants to voice their opinion publicly.

▶ Always ask yourself these questions when you're trying to identify risks: "What might go wrong (risk)? What might help us (opportunity)?"

Project Work Breakdown Structure and Network Diagram

Did you create a work breakdown structure (WBS) for your project? Did you already deal with the network diagram and the critical path of your project? If you can answer both questions with "YES", then I congratulate you. I often only see shrugs and questioning looks when I'm addressing these two essential and often underestimated elements of good project planning.

Many project team members think risk management just concentrate on the risks of the whole project, but that couldn't be further from the truth.

Risk management doesn't just concentrate on the risks of the whole project; a big part of it is also the focus on the identification of risks for each work package and activity. That's why the project work breakdown structure and a network diagram are helpful tools.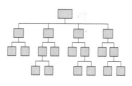

Risks on the Critical Path

Which project work would be most affected by an unforeseen problem? You'll most likely answer: "Wherever the biggest time pressure exists, in combination with a tight schedule."

You have probably already heard about critical paths of a project. The critical path is a path from the beginning to the end of a network diagram that has the lowest sum of all buffer times.

The critical path has major importance when it comes to project plan-

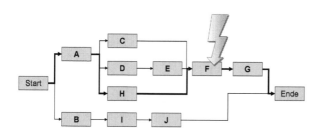

Figure 7: Network Diagram with Risks for Work Packages on the Critical Path

53

ning, as it determines the duration of the project.

Watch out, if on the critical path, something unplanned happens! Particularly risks that threaten work packages on the critical path can wreak great damage if they occur. The completion of the project might be delayed for a significant amount of time. Therefore you should closely examine work packages on the critical path for risk during risk identification. To find further risks you should look for the following in the net-network diagram:

> **The "critical path" is very sensitive to risks.**

- Converging paths: Work packages in the network diagram where multiple paths converge are a lot riskier.

- Resource distribution and skills: Inexperienced project members participating in work packages on the critical path generate risks.

- Dependencies: Dependencies should make sense and be minimized to lower risks.

- Buffers: Hidden buffers in work package or between work packages are a risk that might cause a delay in delivery dates.

Checking the Assumptions

Assumptions in projects always have uncertainties attached to them. If you find out that assumptions made in the project turn out to be false, then there are often more or less difficult problems to be solved.

Assumptions are educated guesses and opinions on which further work in the project and decisions are based on. More often than not, people are optimistic and assume the best-case scenario, while taking on potential risks for the project. "We assume that the law will come into effect in December 2012." If there are some politicians in the parliament that are against it, then the new law might not come into effect after all and a big problem suddenly arises.

Relying on assumptions means generating additional risks for the project, which you should avoid by taking certain measures. This proverb from Benjamin Disraeli is quite fitting in this regard:

"What we anticipate seldom occurs; what we least expected generally happens."

The PMBOK® recommends that the project manager periodically checks the stability of the assumptions. This means: How realistic are the assumptions and are they still valid? What are the consequences if an assumption turns out to be wrong? The project team should always ask these questions, as long as the assumptions are still valid.

As a project manager, one should first pay attention that all assumptions are identified without leaving out any of them. The discussion with the project team or the experts provides further important input regarding the assumptions that have been made and which risks are attached to them.

Assumptions in your project are always potential risks.

Assumptions have to be monitored continuously. This is the only way to have the uncertainties under control. For assumptions that suddenly prove to be invalid, it's important to have contingency measures in place.

When Risks Occur After Project Completion

The project is over, the project manager and the project team have reached their goal. The project was completed within its budget, at the planned date and the specifications were fully met. This success is thoroughly celebrated.

The product is on the market for half a year now. The product manager finds out that the sales numbers are only half as big as projected. The customers aren't accepting the product as expected. After nine months, the company is told that a user of the product has severely injured himself due to a technical defect of the product and the case is likely to go to court.

What happened in this case? During risk identification, the project team focused exclusively on what could go wrong during project execution, i.e., everything that would have endangered the achievement of the project goal, but was less concerned about potential issues after project closure. They have considered a point too little: what could happen if the product is on the market and used? What can jeopardize the success of the product? The period after project closure was probably simply faded.

The following figure shows that the project team's focus is most often only on project execution risks: Time, cost, quality and performance.

The system risks of the finished product, in relation to companies, customers/users and the society are often faded. The system risks are in the areas of profitability, acceptance and safety.

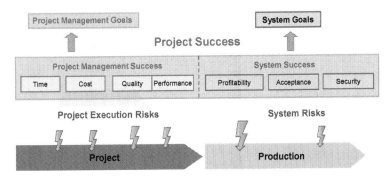

Figure 8: Project Execution Risks and System Risks have a Different Focus

Don't Just Look for Project Execution Risks

Did you also wonder about a project that was successfully completed but still didn't turn out to be a success? I don't want to allege that project managers have a "devil may care" attitude, but anything that might come up "after project closure" is usually no longer very relevant to the project manager and the team. The project manager is managing another project or has returned to the line organization. The sensibility for anything that might come up after "project closure" is often lacking and neglected.

What might happen when the project is finished and the system is in use?

Depending on the nature and the content of a project, far-reaching risks must be considered, in some cases, up to the decommissioning of the project outcome. The risk assessment then goes beyond the scope of the project duration and might include the social environment and beyond the operation of the product, such as the decommissioning or removal of harmful consequences or legacy. The responsibility of the project manager can get a lot bigger this way and extends into the corporate management's sphere of responsibility. The profitability of the project alone is not sufficient as the sole measure of value anymore this way. One has to be concerned about the combination of possible system risks and the resulting consequences that might affect the company's reputation. For example these are:

- the long term success of the customer and company
- the safety for the user and the environment
- the social and biological environmental compatibility

There are two ways to handle these kinds of risks, which go beyond the project duration:

- To include these kind of risks explicitly in the risk assessment.
- To prevent far-reaching negative consequences (or promotion of far-reaching positive consequences) are defined as part of the project goals.

In the following paragraphs I'm addressing the most important system risks, that often don't receive much attention.

Market Risks

The longer a project takes and the higher the competition, the greater the market risk, especially in fast-moving consumer products. It's therefore important to assess market developments as well as the competitors during project execution and to maintain a relationship with future users of the product.

Reputational Risks

The public perception of a company defines its corporate value significantly. It's based partly on executed and neglected acts of the company in the past, as well as the communicated future strategic direction.

A loss of confidence can have a diverse impact on the company. Consequences include a decreasing market share, higher capital costs and the reduction of employer attractiveness.

Security Risks

Security risks are often ignored in projects. For the development of banking and insurance products, they don't play a major role (IT-Security is not implied). In the software industry security risks might be able to cause a loss of life, as for example, for software that controls airplanes. Security risks are always an important topic when it comes to the development of technical products and machines, especially when it comes to product liability claims. Product liability is the area of law in which manufacturers,

Ignored security risks are likely to catch up with you after the project closure!

distributors, suppliers, retailers, and others who make products available to the public are held responsible for the injuries those products cause.

When are You Finished with Risks Identification?

Many project managers think that five identified risks are sufficient enough to return to "normal" project work. This, however, doesn't show project management maturity. You should spare no effort to identify as many risks as possible as quickly as possible. You should also employ multiple risk identification methods in your effort. The sooner the risks are identified, the earlier you're able to define measures against them. Identify risks until you hear truly exceptional risks.

Independent of the method that is used to identify risks – all risks found will be reviewed and evaluated by the project manager and his team.

Before you go one step further in the risk management process, you should be sure that you have spent enough time on identifying risks. You should ask yourself the following questions:

- Is the risk identification worth more time?
- Did we contact all important persons?
- Did we forget to check any documents, specifications, literature, reports or contracts?
- Are there ways and methods to identify risks that we haven't used so far?
- Do we understand the risks enough to be able to analyze and rate them?
- Did we truly give our best when it comes to identifying risks?

▶ Questions in the area of project scope and requirements are often not fully resolved. These uncertainties are often underestimated and can strongly interfere with project progress. "Does training belong to the scope of the project?" Unanswered questions should be resolved before risk identification takes place!

▶ Work packages and activities contain risks. Go through all elements of the work breakdown structure and ask yourself what could go wrong with them.

▶ Risks that are already known at project start should be written down in the project charter. The appropriate actions go directly into first project planning this way.

▶ Look back on completed projects. What kind of problems did you fight there? Ask other experienced project managers and consult the "Lessons Learned" from finished projects.

▶ Look at the assumptions. Assumptions are relevant risks that can influence the project in a strong way. Assumptions should be clearly identified and constantly monitored.

▶ Spend some time identifying system risks, e.g., project risks that might occur after the completion of the project, such as security risks or market risks.

Qualitative Risk Analysis

Objective of the Qualitative Risk Analysis

The objective of the qualitative risk analysis is to determine the probability and the impact of the risks. When you have completed the qualitative risk analysis, you can define for which risks further actions should be taken. Not all risks are very likely to occur and not all of them might have a big impact on the project.

In the qualitative risk analysis, you rate risks on qualitative scales, for example from "very low" to "very high". In quantitative risk analysis however, you're rating risks or their impact on a quantitative scale such as a loss of money in dollars or a loss of time in days.

The objective of a qualitative risk analysis is to:

▦ Provide a qualitative rating of the probability and impact of the risks and opportunities.

▦ Create a shorter list of risks through the determination of critical risks (Top Risks).

▦ Decide for which risks you need to define actions

▦ Determine a go/no-go decision for the project after the risks are rated.

You have to perform the following tasks for the qualitative risk analysis:

▦ Collect all information necessary to rate the risks.

▦ Determine probability and impact of each risk, as well as a possible trigger for the risk.

▦ Determine when and in what kind of intervals the risk can occur.

- Check if the data used for risk identification are still up to date, precise and reliable.
- Create a prioritized list of risks. Determine which risks need to be addressed further in the risk management process (Top Risks).
- Determine the total risk score of the project.

Determine Probability and Impact

The Probability

The first factor that determines the risk of a project is the probability. This expresses the probability that an event (risk or opportunity) occurs. It ranges from 0% (does not occur) to 100% (occurs certainly).

It's relatively easy to determine what the impact of a risk will mean for the project objectives. You only have to imagine the situation after the risk has occurred. Rating the probability can be a bit more difficult though. The two most important reasons for this are subjectivity and a lack of experiences. The evaluation of the probability requires an opinion about future events that haven't occurred yet. Different persons will have a different opinion about the future. There is no right or wrong answer, as the future has yet to come. The subjective opinion is often influenced by many different factors. It should be discussed within the evaluation team and whenever possible, merged into a consensus opinion.

How can you evaluate the probability with a lack of experience? Even experienced project managers and project teams might come across many risks that are very specific to the project and therefore haven't occurred yet and have never been dealt with before. You're likely to get challenged again every time!

There are a few methods which support the quantitative and qualitative risk assessment:

- The Delphi Method
- Monte Carlo Simulations
- The Regression- and Correlation Analysis
- The Probabilistic-Event-Analysis

■ The Program Evaluation and Review Technique (PERT)

If you see this list you might feel a bit dizzy. I won't elaborate any further on these rather complicated methods. I think when you, as a project manager, know and apply the methods described in this book, then you have already done a lot. The additional value of the other methods is quite low in my opinion.

In practice, the probability of the impact is mostly subjectively estimated. If you're doing these tasks with your project team and eventually consult experts, then this is fully sufficient.

The Impact Describes the Possible Damage

The impact describes the possible damage (or benefit) when a risk (opportunity) occurs. The damage or benefit during project execution always has an influence on the four competing factors in project management:

■ Costs

■ Time

■ Quality

■ Performance

On page 55 you read that risks can also occur after the completion of the project. You also have to rate the impact of these so called system risks. System risks have an impact on the following project factors:

■ Profitability

■ Acceptance

■ Safety

Although always one of these seven factors is affected by risks, in the end the damage or benefit always has a monetary consequence. This effect is, however, not always so easy to quantify.

Rating Scales for Probability and Impact

If no rating scales are defined yet in your company, the following tables will provide you an indication for the rating of the probability and the impact. For the impact, the values for schedule, costs and quality/performance are supposed to make the subjective rating a bit easier. It can be useful to convert the percentage values in the table into effective days or dollars to get an even better feeling for the dimensions of "low" and "high".

Rating the Probability

Rating	Interpretation
5 - very high	(80% ... 100%)
4 - high	(50% ... 80%)
3 - moderate	(30% ... 50%)
2 - low	(10% ... 30%)
1 – very low	Rather unlikely (0% ... 10%)

If you rate the probability with 5, then it means that the risk is likely to occur with a high probability. If you reach this conclusion you should take care of the risk immediately, as it could turn into a problem in a short amount of time.

Rating of the Impact

The percentage in the following table should be interpreted with care. A delay of the project duration by 5 to 10 percent can be catastrophic for a project with a contractually defined penalty for non-performance. The impact of the costs can be related to the project budget or to the project budget incl. the revenue from the product over 3 years for example, which makes more sense to me.

Rating	Schedule	Cost	Quality
5 – very high	Delay in delivery >20% (... Days)	Exceedance >20% (...$)	The result of the project is unusable
4 - high	Delay in delivery 10...20% (... Days)	Exceedance 10...20% (...$)	A lower quality is not acceptable
3 - moderate	Delay in delivery 5...10% (...Days)	Exceedance 5...10% (...$)	Important areas are affected
2 - low	Delay in delivery <5% (...Days)	Exceedance <5% (...$)	Only a minor reduction of quality
1 – very low	Delay in delivery is insignificant	Exceedance is insignificant	Barely noticeable differences

Rating Scales with Three Values: Small, Medium, High

According to the comprehensive experience of risk management expert Rita Mulcahy[1], many companies make the big mistake of using a scale for risk analysis, which consists of three parts labeled: "small", "medium" and "high". Why is she against this practice? In the following lines you can find her explanation:

If you only have three options to choose from, how can you separate 10 risks that all have a high probability and a high impact? Even for 30 risks, the three part scale offers a too narrow range to sort risks by their rating. With a wider range, it's easier and faster to rate risks and to put them into a rating matrix. At the same time, you receive a more differentiated picture of the situation, even though it's only a subjective rating. A broad range will also lower the uncertainty when someone wants to rate a risk as "high", but his colleague rates it as "medium". Rita Mulcahy suggests that a scale from 1 to 10 should be used for the rating of probability and impact. I share her opinion. Five part scales, as used by the PMBOK®, already offer more flexibility in comparison to three part scales. If someone claims this is all about spurious accuracy, then he didn't understand the reason behind it. For the sake of simplicity, I'm using a five part scale in this book.

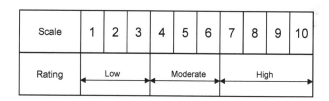

Figure 9: Rating Scale with 10 Steps

Rita Mulcahy PMP, Risk Management – Tricks of the Trade for Project Managers 2003

The Risk Matrix

A good technique to qualitatively analyze and present risks is the risk matrix. It shows the risk rating of each risk to all parties involved in a simple and quick way.

Every risk gets entered into the matrix by its probability and impact. The position in the matrix correlates to the relative importance or, respectively, the risk level of the risk. In the upper right corner in the red boxes, you can find the dangerous risks and in the lower left corner in the white boxes, the least dangerous risks appear. If you're using the risk matrix as management information, then you should limit yourself to the 5 to 8 biggest risks on the matrix, as a large amount of risks might get confusing.

Figure 10 shows the actual position of the risk without response. On page 91 you can find a risk matrix with the actual risk position and the nominal risk position after planning of risk control measures.

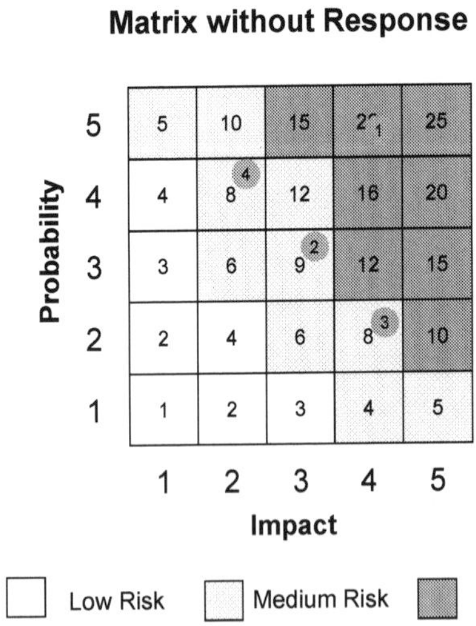

Matrix without Response

Figure 10: Risk Matrix with Risk Ratings

How to Determine Probability and Impact Efficiently

The determination of probability and impact can be a time consuming procedure. If you have to rate 100 risks and each risk has to be evaluated on its own by your team, then the task can take several hours to complete, especially if there are multiple opinions about each risk. Can you imagine the frustration of your team after 15 minutes have passed and only 4 risks have been evaluated? There are better and faster ways to rate risks:

Method 1: Fill out an excel spreadsheet with all risks and let all team members evaluate each risk in the document independently from each other. The median will be calculated automatically and rounded up to the next whole number. This method is fast but has several disadvantages: It's rather boring for the participants and the productivity can suffer due to this fact. Experiences also don't get exchanged between the participants.

Method 2: Here you'll act like judges at an ice skating competition. Your team members get cards with the numbers "1" to "5". The first risk is announced. Every participant puts his card with the number for the rating of the probability into the air within 2 seconds. At the beginning of the meeting, someone is chosen to do the counting and the calculation of the total sum of all numbers for the determination of the median, which gets rounded up to the next whole number. The same thing is done for the impact. This way you won't need more than 30 seconds for each risk.

> **Rate the risks efficiently. Long discussions about them are frustrating.**

Method 1 and 2 have the disadvantage of a lack of communication about each individual rating and a lack of discussion about ratings that deviate strongly from the media.

Method 3: The method with a pin board is the fastest one, according to Rita Mulcahy. You should proceed in the following way:

1. Create a risk matrix with a size of approximately 2m x 2m with 100 boxes (10x10) and put it on the floor so the accessibility is better and it can be read more easily. This makes the meeting a lot easier and more engaging.

2. Distribute the pin board cards with the risks among the team members that have created the cards. The left over cards from various sources should be distributed evenly among the participants.

3. Let the team members put the risks on a matching spot on the risk matrix by their estimated probability and impact.

4. Often not everybody agrees with the individual rating. Let the team members mark the cards with a highlighter that have ratings which they don't agree with, so they can be discussed later on. Surprisingly, it's often only a very few cards that have to be discussed later on.

5. Discuss the marked cards and make adjustments to their rating, if necessary.

6. Determine if any risk needs additional information or clarification and eliminate risks that aren't relevant anymore.

7. Mark the cards with the determined probability and impact, so they can be used later on during the risk management process.

This way you'll be done with the qualitative risk analysis in record time!

Risks with a Very High Impact

If the impact of a risk is rated as very high you should always take action to lower it. This should also be the case if the probability is very low. It's surprising how many project managers tend to simply ignore such risks.

The challenger space shuttle disaster on 28 January 1986 is a good example for this. Many of the team members that were responsible for the start of the space shuttle believed that the probability of the failure of a certain o-ring of the rocket engine was very low. The impact of the failure was very high, though, which was showed by the explosion of the space shuttle that killed all astronauts. The o-rings were unsuitable for very low temperatures – this was known. If the launch had been moved to a day with warmer weather, the disaster could have been avoided.[2]

---

[2] http://en.wikipedia.org/wiki/O-ring#Challenger_disaster

Determining the Risk Score of the Project

The risk score of each risk originates from the multiplication of the probability with the impact. The total risk score of the project is the sum of all risk scores – in the following example, the value 46. If you have identified lots of risks and opportunities, it makes less sense to follow them all in detail during the risk management process. That's why only risks above a certain risk threshold are evaluated further. These risks we call Top-Risks. In the following example, a risk value of 5 and an opportunity value of -5 were chosen as the limit for Top Risks.

Risk Score For Project Saturn				
Risks & Opportunities No.	Probability	Impact	Risk Score P x I	Risk Rank within The Project
1	2	3	6	4
2	1	-3	-3	Not Top
3	2	2	4	Not Top
4	2	4	8	3
5	3	4	12	1
6	2	5	10	2
7	1	3	3	Not Top
8	2	4	8	3
9	1	4	4	Not Top
10 (Opportunity)	2	-3	-6	4
Total Risk Score of the Project			46	

Figure 11: Risk Score for Project Saturn

The total risk score of the project before planning of actions in this example is 46. This key figure is defined before and after planning of actions on a monthly basis. This way the risk trend can be evaluated before and after planning of actions.

The risk score of the project can't be compared to other projects, as every project has a different amount of identified risks. Only if you take the top 5 or the top 10 risks of every project, a qualitative comparison with different projects might be possible.

Further Processing of Non-Top Risks

What do you do with the risks that aren't among the Top Risks and have no actions defined for the case of an occurrence? I recommend that you keep these risks in the risk register and periodically evaluate them again. With the continued development of the project, you'll know more about it and its risks. That's why you should evaluate and rate these risks again. Some risks will evaporate, while others might get more dangerous and eventually rise to the top of the risk register.

Show the Risks on the Network Diagram and the Gantt-Chart

I recommend that you associate each single work packages with the corresponding risk value. Mark the work packages with the highest risk in red and the ones with the lowest risk or no risk in green. This is not always easy, but it might provide you with new insights when you look at the network diagram or the bar chart (Gantt-Chart). If you see the high risk "H" on the critical path as in Figure 12, then you'll most likely be more careful. Work package "H" and "E" with high risks lead to work package "F". What would you do in this constellation? I'd take actions for work package "H" and "E", if possible, to lower the risk or to fully eliminate it. It might make sense to put a time buffer in front of work package "F" to protect it – more so because three paths lead to "F".

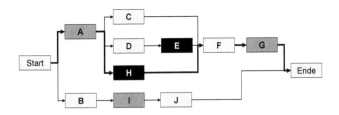

Figure 12: Show Risks in the Network Diagram

An important insight in risk management is the fact that many risks never occur – mainly because they're known. You can use this fact by informing as many stakeholders as reasonable about the identified risks. You have a suitable mean for this with the bar chart. Create a new column in the bar chart with the title "risk score" and enter the risk score for each work package. In the next column it would be best to enter the responsible person for each work package.

Quantitative Risk Analysis or go Direct to Response Planning?

The qualitative risk analysis is completed. You decided to go one step further. Now you need to decide if the next step is the quantitative risk analysis or if you go directly to response planning. You should consider that the quantitative risk analysis is not as important as some people might think. What is more important: To spend more time on risk identification and eventually find more risks or doing a quantitative risk analysis? To make the decision a bit easier for you, I have created the following guidelines:

Continue with the quantitative risk analysis:

- If you believe that you have identified all risks
- If it's worth the time and money on your project
- If you have a project with a high priority and visibility
- If you have a very small tolerance when it comes to costs and schedule

Go directly to response planning:

- If you have a project with a small budget and a short duration
- If you only have little experience in risk management

- ▶ Associate the risks with each work package. This way you can see which work packages are affected by which risks and which are not.

- ▶ Are there any work packages with high risks attached on the critical path? You should pay special attention to such risks and work packages and take actions if it's appropriate.

▶ If a work package is affected by several smaller risks (not top rated risks), it's suddenly a bigger danger for the project. Also, for this work package you should plan actions.

Quantitative Risk Analysis

● ●

The Goal of Quantitative Risk Analysis

The qualitative risk analysis is followed by the quantitative risk analysis. Now we want to know the impact of the risks in dollars and days. The quantitative risk analysis is not the most important part of risk management. The time that you spend on risk identification and the qualitative risk analysis has a much bigger benefit.

With the results of the quantitative risk analysis you can, however, better judge where it makes sense to invest time and money into actions. After the quantitative risk analysis, you'll also be certain how much risk the project really carries. You might be able to find out that risks at large projects might potentially harm your company.

Actually, it would always make sense to do a quantitative risk analysis to get a better feeling for the risks. For small projects, you can refrain from it though, as the effort/benefit ratio of a quantitative risk analysis is not very ideal. If you're in doubt, you should rather use more time for the risk identification and the qualitative risk analysis and leave out the quantitative risk analysis.

Determine Probability and Impact

You already determined the probability during the qualitative risk analysis. There shouldn't be any adjustments necessary, unless you know more about certain risks in the meantime. The probability is often based on subjective estimations. Also the impact can be subjectively estimated.

However, it's often possible to make calculations regarding the impact, as for example: If the safety test doesn't work, then we'll have a delay of one week and a damage of $12,000. The rating quality can be further improved if you take additional time to gather the best possible data.

It might make sense to expand the risk assessment. Then you won't just concentrate on costs and time anymore, but also rate the impact on the quality, or, for example, customer satisfaction.

You'll deal with the following tasks during the quantitative risk analysis:

- Supplement the existing risk register with the qualitatively rated risks with the data of probability and impact:
    - Rate the probability between 0...90% (if not already done).
    - Rate the impact with the effective dollar amounts when the risk occurs.
    - Rate the impact with the effective time scales. Depending on the length of the project, you should choose weeks or days.
- Check the calculated values: "Expected Value of Costs" and "Expected Value of Time" and the corresponding sums at the end of the spreadsheet.
- Determine for which risks actions should be planned.
- Determine for which affected work packages measures should be planned.
- Determine how much the project is likely to cost and how long it's likely to take, if no further measures are taken to lower the risks and to increase the opportunities.

Rating Risks in Dollars and Days

Quantitative risk analysis seems to be a time consuming task, but you already did the biggest preparatory work: risk identification and the qualitative risk analysis. Now it's about getting a feel for the damage a risk really could cause – in dollars and days. In the following table, the probability was determined in percentage and the impact in dollars and days. You should note that risks 2 and 10 are opportunities. You should also pay attention to the fact that a probability of more than 80% is not a risk anymore, but a fact, or respectively a problem, which should be taken care of immediately.

In the last column "Move to Response Planning?" you define whether you are planning measures for the risk or if the risk is only monitored. Define a threshold beyond which the risks have to be added to response planning. In our example all risks with a risk value beyond 2000/-2000 dollars will be added to response planning.

The cost and time risk values are mostly estimates, which is also a reason why you shouldn't look at them as an absolute truth. These values, however, provide a good reference point to the magnitude of the impact in case a risk occurs. Don't get frustrated by the high numbers! You should be motivated instead, to significantly lower the risk of the project with strong actions.

Quantitative Risk Analysis						
Risk	Probability in %	Cost Impact in $	Expected Value of Cost in $	Schedule Impact in Days	Expected Value of Time in Days	Move to Response Planning?
1	25	8'000	2'000	7	1.75	Yes
2	10	-3'000	-300	-4	-0.4	No
3	40	5'000	2'000	5	2.75	Yes
4	25	7'000	1'750	-	-	No
5	60	40'000	24'000	20	12	Yes
6	25	9'000	2'250	10	2.5	Yes
7	10	2'500	250	-	-	No
8	25	20'000	5'000	40	12	Yes
9	10	3'000	300	2	0.2	No
10	40	-10'000	-4'000	-10	-4	Yes
Total expected values			33'250	Time	26.8	

Figure 13: Quantitative Rating of the Risks

Best/Expected/Worst Case Calculation

With the quantitative risk analysis you'll be able to calculate the best/expected/worst case scenario. The probability that the worst case scenario occurs is rather small, but not totally unlikely. The damage however is usually terrifying.

- **The expected case** defines the costs and length of the project if no further actions are taken and all risks and chances occur with their determined probability and impact.

- **The best case** defines the costs and length of the project when no risk occurs and the opportunities occur with a probability of 100%.

- **The worst case** defines the costs and length of the project if all risks occur with a 100% probability and no opportunities occur.

- **The "Boss Case"** defines the costs and length of the project that your project sponsor or boss expects.

Example:

A project costs 600,000 dollars, according to the project plan and lasts 300 days. The risk values are taken from the table on page 75.

What is the best/expected/worst case and boss case for this project? The following table shows the corresponding calculations.

Case	Calculation Dollar	Response Dollar	Calculation Days	Response Days
Best Case	600'000 - (3000+10'000)	587'000	300 -(4+10)	286
Expected Case	600'000 + 33'250	633'250	300+26.8	326.8
Worst Case	600'000 + 94'500	694'500	300+84	384
Boss Case		600'000		300

Figure 14: Best Case/Worst Case Calculation

For the boss, or rather the project sponsor, there is often only the "Boss Case". This means that the project is not supposed to cost a dollar more or last a day longer than previously agreed to. But what are you supposed to do now? With appropriate actions, that aren't supposed to cost anything, you're trying to lower the probability and the impact of the risks, while increasing the opportunities. With good management skills and a portion of luck, the "Boss Case" might be reachable after all!

▶ Interview relevant stakeholders/experts, if possible, to be able to quantify the risks. This is time consuming, though.

▶ When you're quantifying the risks, you shouldn't just look at time and costs, but also at quality and performance (decreased/-increased). This could also strongly influence the success of the project.

▶ Don't forget to analyze the good risks (opportunities).

▶ Mark the work packages with the risk values on the bar chart (Gantt-Chart) or network diagram to get a feeling for the risks on the critical path of the project and to be able to take appropriate measures.

Response Planning

Response Planning for more Security

When planning responses, you define appropriate actions to eliminate or reduce risks at an early stage with the goal to reduce the overall risk of the project. Then you have to implement these actions in a timely manner.

During response planning, you try to reduce the probability and impact of risks and increase the probability and impact of the discovered opportunities. These responses will be documented in the response plan and monitored and adjusted as necessary during project execution. Avoiding or reducing risks increases the chance that you will finish your project on schedule and at planned costs.

> *"If you don't actively attack the risks, they will actively attack you."*
> *(Tom Gilb)*

Tom Gilb gets right to the point: who does not actively encounter risks with firm actions will be surprised by them and will have to work hard for some time. Do not let it get that far! With effective responses for the major risks, your project life will be a lot easier.

In general, there are three types of actions to deal with risk in response planning:

- Do something to eliminate the risk or reduce probability or impact of the risk before something happens (or increase it for opportunities)
- Do something if the risk happens: **Contingency plan**
- Do something if the contingency plan is not effective: **Fallback plan**

The key word in response planning is "appropriateness". The appropriate response for each type of risk is clearly different. For some threats is might be appropriate to eliminate the risk as fast as possible. For other risks the response may be to do nothing and wait and see what happens or you may even consider to cancel the project.

You will deal with the following tasks in the response planning:

1. Change, if possible, the project plan to eliminate risks.
2. Change, if possible, the project plan to reduce the probability and impact of risks.
2. Determine the remaining risks and define actions and responsible risk owners for them.
4. Define emergency and contingency plans if risks occur.
5. Define a contingency reserve (time, money) for identified risks for which no actions have been taken (residual risks).
6. Define a reserve for risks that have not been identified.
7. Repeat the qualitative risk analysis to see whether the new sum of the top risks is below the defined threshold. If this is not the case, continue with response planning.
8. Get the approval of the project sponsor and the relevant stakeholders for the risk response plan and the reserves.
9. Together with the senior management, make a project go/no go decision based on the results of the response planning.

Response Planning is Teamwork

How do you start the process of response planning best? How much time should you employ? How much should the actions cost? Who participates in them? For all these issues, there are no clear answers. The methods, participants and the necessary time and costs are highly dependent on project size, complexity of the project, the available resources and the priority of the project. You should have already defined in the risk management plan how to proceed in response planning. For small projects, one meeting with the project team members and key stakeholders is usually enough. After a 30-minute brainstorming session, you could develop a rough response plan. For larger projects, you will need more meetings, for example, additional meetings with specialists for particular issues, with relevant stakeholders or with sub-suppliers. Recommended methods for response planning are brainstorming sessions, interviews, surveys via e-mail or combined variants.

In contrast to risk identification, where experience and analytical skills in risk analysis is rather helpful, at response planning, creativity is demanded. Often, the rather quiet participants come up with creative ideas at response planning. Note that during the brainstorming no ideas should be evaluated. Animate your colleagues to share crazy ideas too. Every idea counts! Crazy ideas often provide material for practical actions. You can sort out the really impossible ideas later.

At response planning, creativity is demanded.

Risk Response Strategies

The nature of risks in your project will be very different. Therefore, you should check at response planning which risk response strategy is the most appropriate for the particular risk.

The chosen response can then either act on the cause or the effect of the risk, or both. The following figure shows the various risk response strategies.

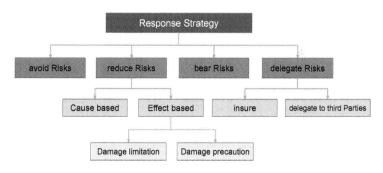

Figure 15: Different Response Strategies for Response Planning

Avoiding risks: Eliminate the danger of a risk by eliminating the cause of the risk or reduce the probability of the risk to zero. One obvious way to do this, is not performing an activity that carries a risk. This can be achieved through clever rescheduling or, for example, by omitting a functionality of the product, which poses great risks.

Avoiding risks seems to be the best strategy for all risks. You should note, however, avoiding risks may also mean losing potential benefits that you would achieve taking the risks.

Some risks can be avoided at the beginning of the project by clearly specifying project objectives and requirements. Comprehensive information gathering, clear communication and involvement of relevant stakeholders also helps to eliminate risks. More possibilities

> **Avoiding risks is not always the best strategy.**

are: Reduction of the project scope to avoid high-risk activities, planning of additional resources and time, and avoiding unreliable suppliers. Each eliminated risk is a success!

"It is better to avoid a risk, than managing it" (Harvey Levine)

Reducing risks: Take up measures that reduce the probability and/or impact of the risk. The measure can either have an effect on the cause of the risk (cause-based risk reduction) or directly impact the risk (impact-based risk reduction). The impact-based risk reduction could be further divided into damage limitation and damage precaution. The cause-based measures include, for example, coaching measures for the project manager or more intensive tests of the software at an earlier stage of the project. The impact-based measures include, for example, special safety systems, which turn off immediately in serious cases, certain equipment (damage precaution) or sprinkler systems in buildings that limit the damage (damage limitation).

Other typical measures to reduce the risks are seat belts and air bags in cars. They have to avoid or decrease injuries in the case of an accident. However, there are people who say that this provides a false sense of security to the driver. In this case, it is better to take measures to ensure that the driver does not cause an accident. That is dealing with the cause rather than with the effect. One measure of this would be a spinning course, so that the driver controls his vehicle better.

Delegating risks: This means that you give the risk with all possible consequences and the responsibility for reduction measures to third parties who can manage risks better than you. This could be an insurance company or a sub-supplier. Risk delegation is useful for risks with direct financial implications. This usually costs a premium. Therefore, the supplier charges a risk premium in his calculations and the insurance company will ask for an insurance premium. Risks are often delegated in contractual terms, as in the liability or limitation of liability or any granting of guarantees or with fixed-price contracts. To delegate risks to sub-suppliers can be problematic in some cases, because you will depend

> **Often, it is better to control the risks yourself than assigning them to somebody else.**

on the sub-suppliers. If the sub-supplier does not control the risk, then you may suffer from that as well. Therefore, it is often better to control the risks yourself.

Bearing risks: "If it happens, it happens." The project team has decided, after extensive review, to bear the risk themselves and take no action. To bear risks yourself is a reasonable strategy, for example, for small risks, but also for risks, where the measures would be (e.g. an insurance) more expensive than the potential damage would cost if it occurs. It could also be that many possible measures generate too many secondary risks and therefore will not be considered. To bear actively yourself means that the project team will still work out a contingency plan in case that the risk occurs. While bearing passively yourself means that nothing will be done. If something happens, then we will have to bear the damage.

The contingency strategy: You cannot find this strategy in Figure 15. At this strategy, you only act if certain events happen that herald the occurrence of the risk. Therefore, for certain risks, it is useful to define actions only when the occurrence of risks is announced by early warning signals. The trigger for actions might include the failing of important achievements, or a revision of the law that is being moved by the parliament.

Cope with Risks in Four Stages

The overall risk of your project includes the identified risks and the not identified risks. Against the identified risks (known unknowns), you can do something; the not identified risks (the unknown unknowns) you do not know and will be, as tragic as it is, your "destiny".

You should implement the acquainted risk management strategies when planning responses systematically with the following stages.

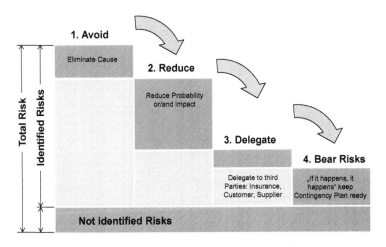

Figure 16: Cope with Risks in Four Stages

Stage 1 – Avoiding risks: Define actions to eliminate the risk. This is achieved by eliminating the cause of the risk or reducing the likelihood of the risk to zero.

Stage 2 - Reducing risks: Take actions to reduce the probability and/or impact of the risk. In the event that the risk should occur after all, you can define a contingency plan.

Stage 3 - Delegating risks: Delegate the risk with all the possible consequences and the responsibility for reducing actions to third parties who can manage the risks better than you. This may be, for example, an insurance company or a sub-supplier.

Stage 4 - Bearing risks: You bear the risk with all the consequences yourself. At actively bearing, you define a contingency plan in the case that the risk occurs. At passively bearing you do not do anything. If the risk occurs, then you are just unlucky and bear the damage!

It would be ideal if you could apply Stage 1 for each risk – eliminate all risks – and you are in peace! This, of course, is our most desired dream. For most risks, you are likely to use Stage 2. For critical risks, you should have a contingency plan ready, if the defined actions show no or too little effect. Even if the contingency plan has too little effect, then you are lucky if you still have a fallback plan ready.

> **For critical risks, you should have a contingency plan ready.**

Risk response strategies for opportunities

Stage 1 - Exploiting opportunities (instead of avoiding): Define actions to ensure that the opportunity occurs definitely. The actions try to influence the cause of this opportunity.

Stage 2 - Improving opportunities (instead of reducing): Use appropriate actions to improve the probability and/or the impact of opportunities. Thus, a small opportunity becomes a great one.

Stage 3 – Keeping or sharing opportunities (instead of delegating): Use of potential opportunities for yourself, or sharing them, rather than leaving them up to others (completely) or share opportunities with another partner who has better opportunities to influence them.

Stage 4 – Accepting opportunities (instead of bearing them): This strategy is mostly used for small opportunities or if there is no meaningful or economical possibility to improve the opportunity. Under these circumstances, it is best doing nothing and rejoicing if the opportunity still occurs.

The Contingency Plan

A contingency plan helps if a risk occurs despite risk reduction measures. Also, at risks, where you have not defined measures (residual risks), a contingency plan in case of emergency may be useful.

The Fallback Plan

The fallback plan defines alternative responses and will start, when the risk occurs and the contingency plan is not effective, i.e. if it has too little or no effect at all.

Trigger for Responses

"Where a ball rolls, a child will follow!" This proven tip from traffic safety can be applied in risk management.

A trigger is an early warning signal that tells the project manager and the risk owner that a risk has occurred or is about to occur. Upon arrival of the trigger signal, the risk owner initiates the defined measures or emergency measures.

For almost every risk, there is an early warning sign. No later than at response planning, should you try to find early warning signals that warn of critical events. Early warning signals count as warning signs for the experienced project manager, sometimes long before the actual risk occurs. Particularly at risk, where no immediate measures can be implemented, triggers play an important role. For these risks often emergency measures are established, which are set off by defined triggers. Especially in monitoring of risks, risk owners have to pay attention to the triggers. Once a trigger occurs, the team member has to take certain actions to reduce or avoid any potential damage.

The answers to the following questions will help you and your team members determine the triggers:

- What will happen right before the risk occurs?
- What can we measure before the risk is about to occur?
- What will we know when the risk is about to occur?

Procedure when Planning Responses

1. Change the project plan to **eliminate** risks.
2. Plan actions to **reduce** the probability and/or impact of risks and adjust the project plan, if necessary.
3. **Delegate** risks and measures to third parties, e.g., an insurance company or a sub-supplier.

4. Determine which risks remain (residual risks) which you will have to **bear**.
5. Determine risk owners for the residual risks.
6. Create, if useful, a contingency plan for the residual risks and a **fallback plan** if necessary.
7. Determine what secondary risks have been created and define contingency and fallback plans if useful.
8. Confirm that the contingency and fallback plans have less impact than the risks, and the impact of secondary risks are not greater than the original risks.
9. Define a contingency reserve for the residual risks.
10. Define a management reserve for the unknown risks.
11. Describe all actions in detail in the response plan.
12. Repeat the qualitative risk analysis to see if the new risk score of the project is below the defined threshold. If not, then proceed with response planning.
13. Repeat the quantitative risk analysis to see if the new risk score of the project is below the defined threshold in dollars or days. If not, then proceed with response planning and adjust the reserves, if necessary.
14. Gain approval for the response plan and the reserves from management/project sponsor or the steering committee.
15. Make a Go/No-Go decision for the project with the senior management/project sponsor, based on the results of response planning.
16. Continue with the risk management process and implement the defined actions in a timely manner.

For smaller/less complex projects, you can omit the procedures 12 and 13.

When choosing a risk response strategy, you should consider the following:

▶ The strategy should work in a timely manner. That means, there should be enough time to implement the actions.

▶ The effort should be adjusted to the danger of the risk. Do not spend more on the actions, as the impact of the risk would cost if it occurs.

▶ One action can contribute to several risks.

▶ Involve the project team, the project sponsor and other stakeholders when selecting the response strategy.

▶ For critical risks, you should get the approval for the response strategy from senior management/project sponsor or the steering committee.

Define Actions in Detail

Actions should be defined in a way that they can be planned specifically and the execution can be monitored. Often, actions are not defined specifically enough and are defined without a time reference or the detailed planning just exists in the mind of the project manager or the sub-project managers. In this case, a great

> **Actions should be defined as detailed as possible.**

danger exists that the actions will be implemented ad hoc, or possibly not at all. Non-specific response plans leads to little confidence and hamper project monitoring significantly. Make it better!

You should consider the following things when defining actions:

- Describe the planned actions in detail.
- Set clear implementation deadlines and budgets for the actions and include the actions in the project plan.
- Define clear responsibilities for the implementation of the actions.
- When planning actions, also consider the work packages or activities with the greatest risks, especially the ones on the critical path of the project.
- Describe actions in the same list/database (the risk register) as the risks. This way you do not lose track.

Who Decides on the Actions?

Normally, the project manager will solely decide in his own competence on the actions. For certain actions, it is wise to discuss them with the project sponsor, the steering committee or the executive management and maybe leave the decision up to them. This relates to actions for very big risks, but also specific risks, which could, for example, damage the business reputation. You should also present risks to the project sponsor and the steering committee, for which no actions can be defined, but which can cause high damage if they occur.

You take the decision depending on the location of the risk in the risk matrix.

- Risks in the white area: decision by project manager
- Risks in the yellow area: decision by project manager/ project sponsor

- Risks in the red area: decision by project sponsor/ steering committee/executive management

Who is responsible for the risk?

At the latest during response planning, one risk owner should be determined for each risk. Often this will be done by the work package managers or the person responsible for the specific activity. A work package may be affected by various risks and will therefore have various risk owners, if appropriate.

The risk owner must be involved in response planning of his risks. Only then, can he be aware of the responsibility for the implementation of the actions. The risk owner initiates the planned risk reduction actions at a specified time and continuously monitors his risks. If a risk materializes, he must ensure that any existing contingency plan will be implemented in accordance with risk response planning.

Define a risk owner for each risk.

The Risk Response Plan

In practice, you can see different types of response plans – very comprehensive ones with all the details to very scarce solutions in which not even the relationship of the actions to the risk is evident. I believe that all risk data, this includes response planning, should exist in an MS Excel list, a database or project management software and should not be scattered in several different lists and files. This facilitates considerably the monitoring and control of risks and measures. The risk response plan is only a supplement to the existing risk register with additional columns.

Responses are not for free!

The existing risk register should be complemented by the following additional information for response planning:

- Response plan for all top risks
- Evaluation of probability and impact of risks after to response planning
- Risk rank in the risk register before and after response planning
- Contingency and fallback plan, including their triggers
- Name of the risk owner

The Risk Matrix after Response Planning

You have already become acquainted with the first risk matrix of the following figure on page 66. In the second matrix, you cannot only see the risks associated with the current position (actual position), but also the new location of the risks if the planned responses have an effect (target position). Focus on the five to eight biggest Top-Risks – more risks in the matrix would be too confusing.

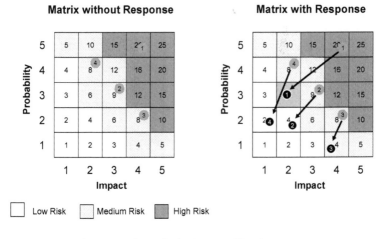

Figure 17: Risk Matrix Before and After Response Planning

Response Planning with External Orders

Risks, which are the responsibility of your sub-suppliers or your external clients, should not be underestimated, because your project depends on them and the risks are largely out of your control. If your counterparty does not have control of the risks, then you are likely to suffer too. Therefore, it is often better to control the risks yourself. Very often this is not possible, and it is not useful to develop everything for yourself.

How can risk management help you specifically for external orders? For the rough initial evaluation of the risk situation, predefined checklists are a great help. Then, a detailed contract review with the help of checklists can be implemented. For large contracts, it is necessary to call in contract specialists of your legal department. During the contract review, you will find terms that will be a risk for you. Also, you may define additional terms in order to reduce your risk and to increase your opportunities, but also to appropriately distribute opportunities and risks between client and contractor. A contract should never be defined and concluded without a risk analysis and contract review!

Reserves for Risks

Actions to prevent risks usually cost money and time. But where do you get the money and the time? Everything is already planned! Surely, you remember: During the whole project execution, you will identify risks and plan appropriate measures, if necessary. Also, unknown risks will occur. Therefore, you will have to plan a contingency reserve already at project start – otherwise, you will go and ask your project sponsor for more budget or more time every second week.

Who does not plan reserves in his project or who hides the reserves "invisibly" in some work packages, works negligently! As hard as it sounds, a serious project manager plans defined reserves clearly.

How to Plan Reserves Right

You cannot identify all risks in your project, even if you try hard. Therefore, reserves have to be created for unidentified risks, to finance possible contingency actions, if they occur.

Reserves are a time and/or cost amount that is added in the project plan for risks. A management reserve is created for risks that are not identified during risk identification, which can lead to unexpected expenses or work. For identified risks for which no responses have been defined, contingency reserves are created. These are often associated with a separate work package in the WBS (work break down structure). Reserves are only for work that exists within the defined project scope, they are not intended for additional project scope.

- **Management Reserve:** For not identified risks (the unknown unknowns)
- **Contingency Reserve:** For identified risk (the known unknowns) for which no actions have been defined

Reserves are only meant for unexpected events. If actions are defined for risks, then they are planned like any other activity in the project plan and have a budget.

Reserves are presented clearly and openly and are not a hidden buffer. Now, many of you might say that these are the first items that are deleted from the budget by the senior management. Therefore, it is often determined that the reserves are under the control of the project sponsor or the senior management. They only become part of your project budget if they are distributed effectively.

The Schedule Reserve

The schedule reserve is a pre-planned time reserve (buffer time) in the project plan, either at critical points in the network diagram and/or at the end of the project. This reserve will also be clearly communicated and is under the control of the senior management or the steering committee.

Buffer time within work packages must be distinguished from the schedule reserve. It corresponds to the time that an activity or a work package may be delayed, without having any impact on the overall project duration.

Buffer - Security for the Unexpected

Buffers are for the unexpected in project execution. They are implemented in financial, temporal or qualitative terms in the project plan. Most commonly, the term is used for scheduling. Financial buffers are also common, but they are rarely named as such. Usually, financial buffers are implemented in the project calculation as so-called "dummy" positions. Buffers should not be hidden in any positions, work packages or under other designations. Buffers should be clearly identified as reserves! This improves the acceptance of reserves and the transparency between senior management and the project manager.

Reserves are no hidden buffers!

▶ Define actions in detail and time-based.

▶ Adjust actions according to the impact or seriousness of the risk. Avoid spending more money on reducing the risk than it would cost if it materializes.

▶ Involve the project team and other stakeholders with their expertise in response planning

▶ During the brainstorming session, some strange, utopian or ridiculous responses might be proposed. Such proposals often lead, in a derived form, to very good actions.

▶ Define monetary and time reserves for responses in your project plan. Time reserves are especially valuable on the "critical path".

Risk Monitoring and Control

• •

The Goal of Risk Monitoring and Control

During Monitoring and Risk Control, the risk response plan will be implemented and the evaluation of the risks in the risk register will be periodically checked. Identified risks and residual risk will be continuously monitored and new, changed and no longer existing risk identified. An essential task is to monitor the defined actions and its implementation. Additionally, it is advisable to continuously evaluate the risk process effectiveness throughout the project.

At this step of risk management, the result of risk analysis and response planning becomes visible. Now it is all about realizing the benefits of these steps. If in the previous steps you spent enough time with the project team and stakeholders and applied good project management, then this step will be much easier.

Are the Risks Still Present or Did they Already Become a Problem?

Risks vary with the maturity of the project. New risks emerge, identified risks disappear and planned actions are implemented. Risk monitoring and control starts exactly at this point. This process step provides important information to assist in effective decisions making – before risks occur.

As mentioned at the beginning of the book, you really cannot manage risks. Consequently, you cannot control uncertainties, which may or may not occur. But yet, risk monitoring and control is an important part of the risk management process. Risk monitoring is continuously check-ing whether the identified risks are still there and if its probability or impact has changed. You also check whether the defined actions still "fit" and how they should be adjusted to the possible new risk situation. An ongoing activity throughout the whole risk management process is, of course, the identification of new risks. If risks change or measures do not work as they should, then the risk management interferes with correc-tive responses.

How to Effectively Monitor Risks

In risk monitoring you check whether the defined risks are still up-to-date and accurately rated. Moreover, you monitor whether the measures are implemented as planned by the risk owner and if they are effective.

In monitoring the risks you check if the probability, the impact or the cause of the risk has changed in the meantime. Maybe you are lucky and find out during monitoring that a risk has disappeared and therefore no longer exists.

In monitoring the actions, you check whether the planned actions are still appropriate, the action plan is executed as planned and already im-plemented actions reduce the risks effectively. Not only are the triggers monitored, which can set off an emergency plan, but the residual risks, for which no measures have been defined, are also monitored and, if necessary, re-evaluated. One consequence of this re-evaluation could be that a residual risk suddenly becomes one of the top risks and needs clearly defined actions.

A continuous activity throughout the risk management process is the identification of new risks. If risks change or actions do not work as they should, then risk management interferes with corrective responses.

You cannot pay the same attention to all risks. Therefore, I suggest: Fo-cus at risk monitoring on the top 5 risks. Spend 70% of the time on the top 5 risks and 30% of the time on the other 20 or 50 risks.

Risk monitoring involves the following activities:

- Check if the probability, the impact or the cause of the risk has changed in the meantime.
- Check if the actions have been implemented as planned.
- Check if the implemented actions work as expected. If not, adjust the actions or define new actions.
- Check if the assumptions used in the project are still valid, or if they have changed.
- Check if the risk exposure of the project has changed (trend analysis).
- Monitor the residual risks and evaluate them again, if needed.
- Monitor if a risk trigger has occurred or is about to occur, or if thresholds are exceeded.
- Determine if risks, that were not identified in advance, have occurred.
- Check if the defined reserves last until the end of the project.

Manage the Critical Path with the Highest Risks

You have already become acquainted with the critical path on page 53. It is the path from the beginning to the end of the network diagram, on which the sum of all the buffer times is minimal. From experience you know that you have to pay close attention on this path during project monitoring – especially when work packages are threatened by risks. From the risk management perspective, there is a second critical path, the path with the highest risks. You will recognize this path when you assign the risks to the respective work packages. And if on this path the buffer vanished through occurring risks, it could quickly become the new critical path of the project.

Monitor the Triggers

You already learned about triggers in planning of actions. Can you remember the following proverb: "Where a ball rolls, a child follows!" Is a ball rolling somewhere? The triggers should be continuously monitored by the risk owner. If such an early warning signal announces that the risk is about to occur, then the risk owner has to implement the predefined actions or emergency actions according to the plan. Only then can a potential loss be reduced or avoided.

Monitoring the Risk Level of the Project

At project team meetings or risk reviews, the risks are newly evaluated, qualitatively and quantitatively. Risks that no longer exist are eliminated, and new risks are added. During risk monitoring, it is good to know how the risk level has changed for the sub-projects but also the total project. The risk level of the project changes with the duration of the project and should steadily decrease towards the end of the project because uncertainties become certainties. These changes of the risk degree can be displayed in a line diagram according to the following figure.

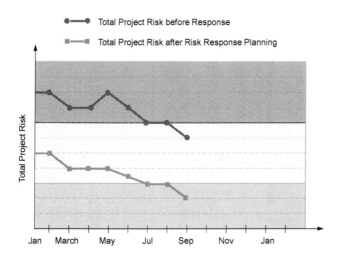

Figure 18: Trend History of Project Overall Risk Before/After Response Planning

Monitoring the Reserves

You should be careful with the reserves. Everyone would just love to access this "free" money pot. That can become a problem, because if the reserves are consumed, it is often difficult to find more money.

Therefore, the status of reserves should be monitored periodically and should be communicated openly and honestly – best with a "burn down" line graph. An example of such a line graph is shown in the following figure. If your project is half done and 80% of the reserves are consumed, then you have a problem that you should discuss with the project sponsor.

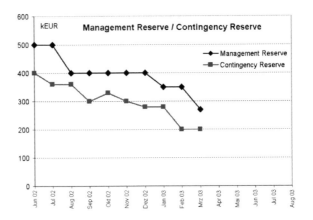

Figure 19: Trend History of Management and Contingency Reserve

Risk Control

An important but often neglected area is risk control. When controlling a project you need a plan, which allows you to compare the actual performance of the project. When deviations are detected, corrective actions must be initiated to get the performance back to its planned results. That sounds relatively trivial, but very often you cannot find a suitable or current plan, which allows you to compare the current performance. Therefore, active project control is a rare activity in projects.

It is quite similar with risk control. But you have to note something: You cannot manage risks (uncertainties)! In risk management it is therefore all about managing and monitoring actions. This means that if risks change or defined actions do not work as assumed, then you must do something, so control and correct

Risk control means: Monitoring and control measures.

the direction. In risk control, it is rational to include the project sponsor and, when it comes to "delicate" actions, also the steering committee. For "normal" operational control, the project manager and his team have enough authority.

At risk monitoring and control, you should consider the following methods and activities:

- Make risks a hot topic at the weekly project status meeting.

- In monthly risk reviews meetings monitor risks and actions and adjust the actions as needed or define new actions.

- Monitor the triggers because triggers are important releases to control measures.

- Also monitor the residual risks and adjust their valuation, if necessary.

- The PMO or other outside experts should perform risk management audits to see if your risk management is implemented effectively.

- Also monitor risks for which no measures have been taken (residual risks).

Risk Reviews/Risk Management Audits

Reviews and audits are two important quality assurance measures in the project environment. Often, however, these two methods are mentioned in the same context. Therefore, I find it necessary to describe these two similar methods briefly and show their differences in their application.

Risk Reviews

With each day of project execution, the environment of the project changes. You learn more and become smarter (hopefully!). This new knowledge must be incorporated into the risk management activities. Therefore, detailed risk reviews should be performed with the project team periodically, for example monthly, or for short complex projects after the completion of a project phase or every two weeks.

Risk reviews are periodic measures of the project manager, which pursue the following objectives:

- Check the existing risks and opportunities: Is the description and evaluation still correct? Do risks cease to apply?
- Search new risks and opportunities in teamwork, based on new knowledge.
- Check if residual risks (risk without responses) have changed and what responses are now necessary.
- Check if defined actions are still valid, if they are implemented and also effective.
- Adjust actions based on new knowledge, among other things, to increase their effect.
- Check if the risk management activities are effective or whether adjustments of the processes are necessary.

Especially the point of new risks should not be neglected. New risks can arise, for example, because of project changes or changes of the environment. A glance at currently ongoing or future activities could also provide information on emerging risks. Any changes of risks require a new qualitative and/or quantitative risk analysis and possibly a new prioritization of risks. It is important that risk reviews are no substitute for the agenda point "Risks" of the weekly project status meetings. Schedule risk reviews in the project plan, so that they cannot "be forgotten".

Risk Management Audits

Risk management audits are a quality assurance measure of the Project Management Office (PMO) or the internal auditors. In risk management audits, auditors check whether the defined risk management process for projects implement the required activities. Important points are:

- Continuity of risk management activities
- Used methods for risk identification
- Quality of discovered risks: Instead of risks, only facts or current problems, for example, were identified?
- Which parties were involved in risk identification?
- Quality of the evaluation and documentation of risks
- Risk communication
- Effectiveness of monitoring and control and implementation of measures

Risk management audits should be performed on all projects of the project portfolio. However, often there is a lack of staff capacity. Therefore, the auditors will have to limit to a few selected projects. The main focus should be at the most important strategic projects. Risk management audits provide a clear signal for the project team: This issue is taken seriously within the company. "My project could probably be the next one." Therefore, from time to time a non-strategic project should be analyzed. When a company introduces risk management audits, it automatically promotes the compliance of the risk management rules. At the same time, this increases the risk management culture within the company.

Risk Management and Project Control

Risk management and project control are two very different areas of project management. Project control continuously checks whether the financials, schedule and project content goals are met. In this process, achieved results (ACTUAL Values) are compared with the PLANNED Values. Then, deviations are analyzed and actions are defined and implemented. Project control is a downstream activity and focuses mainly on the past. Risk management, on the other hand, focuses on the future. It behaves like a forward-looking radar that searches for dangers in the uncertain and unclear future. The radar does not only look for risks, but also opportunities that could generate additional value for the project. Project control deals with the past; risk management deals with the future.

Project control also deals, in an extended approach, with the controlling of resources, quality and also risks. Therefore, monitoring and controlling of risks and actions is also a part of project control. Because of that, you should see risk management activities as an important part of project control. Thus, the results from risk management flow into project control and should be part of the project control report.

Risk Communication and Documentation

● ●

Risk Communication

Risk Communication Reflects the Corporate Culture

"Communicating risks could jeopardize your project!" This statement really has a kernel of truth, because risk-communication highly depends on the corporate culture, but also of the risk culture, i.e. the way how senior management and employees in the company deal with risks. The appropriate risk communication not only depends on these two aspects, but also from different and often covert interests of the stakeholders.

The communication of project risks is a central element throughout the whole risk management process. Nevertheless, it often involves political explosiveness of how and to whom one communicates which risks. Is it really rational to communicate openly all of the risks before starting the project and also during the project? This question I can only answer with a simple "Yes". The open and honest communication between all project involved parties and in particular with the senior management is essential for an effective risk management. Only if honesty and trust exists between all stakeholders, can risk management develop to its fullest potential.

> **An open and honest risk communication is a requirement for an effective risk management.**

Open and Honest Communication Lowers Risks

A good project manager keeps his stakeholders up to date on project status. A regular communication of risks to the relevant stakeholders can result in an improved cooperation, more understanding, more recognition, better support and ultimately an improved project performance.

Risks can be communicated to stakeholders using the following methods/tools:

- Monthly project status report
- Steering committee meeting
- Risk response plan
- Risk reports

The key stakeholder for the project is the project sponsor. At least once a week he should be informed about the status of the project. When it comes to measures for critical risks or if significant risks are about to materialize, the communication with the project sponsor is very important. Communication with stakeholders is also important to peri-

Inform stakeholders regularly about the risks.

odically check the acceptance level of risk or the risk tolerance. This depends on the nature of the project itself, but also on the stakeholders.

The risk appetite of stakeholders or the organization may change very quickly due to various factors inside or outside the company. This implies, for example, an adaptation of the response planning.

Risks - An Ongoing Topic in the Project

Project risks should also be discussed repeatedly within the project team. Does your project team have individuals who try to make things prettier than they really are? They do not want to cause the project manager any problems ... until it's too late. Therefore, it is important that within the project team an open communication culture prevails and project risks are not an unpopular topic. However, it is still worthwhile to establish an anonymous reporting channel. Team members and stakeholders should have the opportunity to report risks without stating the name.

Project risks should be a fixed point on the agenda of the weekly project status meetings. Ask your project team about the status of implementation of actions and their effect, whether the risks have changed, if new risks have emerged, or if existing risks have disappeared. At monthly "big" project meetings or at risk reviews, you should deal in detail with the risks. This is the base for risk controlling and further management activities.

An honest and open communication of project risks as well as its visibility force every stakeholder to think involuntarily. Thus, you automatically reduce the overall risk of the project.

Communicating Reserves

Usually, people do not like to communicate time or budget reserves. As you have read on page 92, reserves, on the one hand, are communicated clearly and openly in project planning and on the other hand after planning of actions for risks. Reserves are not some kind of hidden buffer. Therefore, it is often determined that the reserves are under the control of the project sponsor or senior management. They become part of your budget (baseline) only when they are effectively distributed. Precisely for this reason, the state of the reserves and their use should be communicated periodically to key stakeholders. The status of reserves is best displayed in a trend graph, just like on page 100. The use of reserves can be represented in a chart, for example in an MS Excel list.

Risk Documentation

The "official" documentation of project risks is in most companies determined by the corporate risk management or the Project Management Office (PMO). These boards also determine how risks have to be reported. Often, all data generated in the process of risk management are saved in an MS Excel file, database or enterprise project management software. Specific risk management software is usually not necessary.

The risks will normally appear in the following documents:

- MS Excel file or database with all risk data
- Risk management report for the project sponsor, steering committee and possibly other boards
- Project status report with the TOP-5 risks, their evaluation and measures
- Meeting minutes of the project status meeting: agenda point risks
- Reporting of the project portfolio management to the corporate management
- Documentation of the corporate risk management: category project risks

When documenting risk data, it is important for you, as a project manager, to have a master database. For small projects, a simple Microsoft Excel file suits best. For big projects, a simple database system can be helpful. Special risk management software is not required. Tools for risk management are often included in good corporate project management software.

All risk data should derive from this master file and then be included in the project status report or risk report for example. Sometimes you can see that the sub-project manager keeps a separate project risk and actions list for the sub-project's "minor" risks, in-

All risk information should be saved at a central location.

dependent from the master file. It also happens that the measures for the risks are described in the master file. The exact implementation, however, will then be described in other documents that have no link to the master file. This, of course, is not ideal. You should only use one database for all risk data.

Make all risk management information easily accessible to all project stakeholders to identify additional risks and to increase the awareness of risks. To access previous risk information in the course of the project, you should version the risk register and periodically archive it.

The following figure shows schematically an easy way to document risks and measures in an MS Excel list.

Risk Description Cause/Risk/Impact	Qualitative Risk Analysis	Quantitative Risk Analysis				Response Planning	

Figure 20: Simple Excel List with All Risk Information

▶ Risks should be a top subject for every project team meeting: Checking existing risks, checking the validity and effectiveness of actions and identifying new risks.

▶ If you place the TOP Risks in the project status report prominently, you automatically reduce the probability of occurrence of the risks.

▶ Do not forget to document and monitor risks for which no actions have been taken

▶ Inform your stakeholders regularly about the risks and the taken actions

▶ Save any risk information in one central location.

How to Encourage Team Involvement

Risk management is team work. Only if your entire project team is actively involved can the full potential of risk management be utilized. As a project manager, it is not always easy to convince the project team that risk management has a high value to the project. "Just extra time, a theoretical game – we are practical men though. We have other priorities!" You hear these and similar statements often. If you, as a project manager, are convinced that systematic risk management will help your project, then you already have an important basis to motivate your team. Try to encourage your team using a combination of the following steps[3]:

Mandate it: Insist that a structured risk management process must be implemented on your project. As a project manager, you have the authority to do that. While it is not the whole answer, it sometimes helps to tell people what to do. Refer to your company's procedures, which include a risk process, and explain that there is really no choice.

Simplify it: Risk management need not be complicated. Make the process as simple as possible without compromising effectiveness. Minimize the overhead for the team, keep risk meetings short and focused, and only collect information that you intend to use.

Normalize it: Explain to your team that managing risk is a "normal project task" and it is not an option. Plan and review risk responses the same way as other project tasks, and expect your team to treat them just like any other task.

Demonstrate it: The project manager should lead by example, and be a role model for the team. If you show that you are serious about identifying and managing risk, and actively do it yourself, the team is more likely to follow your example.

Use it: When risk reports are written and forgotten, the team will learn that risk management is not important. But where the direction and strategy of the project is adjusted in the light of risk information, people will see that their efforts make a difference to how the project is run.

Update it: If the risk register is produced once and never updated, or agreed responses are not reviewed and monitored, the risk assessment

[3] Dr. David Hillson PMP FAPM, Encouraging Team Involvement, November 2006

will quickly become outdated and useless. Ensuring that current risk exposure is understood emphasizes the importance of the risk process.

Celebrate it: Look for proof that risk management has tackled a threat so that a problem was avoided, or evidence that a potential opportunity has been converted into a real advantage. Record these successes and tell people about them. Success breeds success.

"Pull" it: Seek the support and buy-in of senior management. When the steering committee or the sponsor asks for risk information as part of the project governance, the team will know that it matters.

Using these points, the project team will understand how important risk management is for you, and it will become encouraged to take risk management seriously and also apply it for themselves - because it works!

The 10 Key Points in Project Risk Management

I congratulate you. You have made it this far! In this book you have read a lot about project risk management. Perhaps you may now think: "If I have to implement it all, then my project will never finish". Therefore, I recommend that you implement as much and spend as much time as is necessary for your project. If you implement the following 10 key points, then you have done a lot:

1. At the beginning of the project, train the project team in risk management.
2. Involve the entire project team in risk management activities.
3. Go through the risk management process not only once, but periodically.
4. Describe the risks in the cause/risk/impact format.
5. Try to identify opportunities.
6. Use different methods for risk identification, such as brainstorming sessions, interviews and checklists.
7. Describe risks and actions in detail.
8. Monitor risks and actions periodically - at best, carry out weekly project status meetings and periodic risk reviews.
9. Focus on the top 5 risks. Spend 70% of the time on the top 5 risks and 30% of the time on the other 20 or 50 risks.
10. You do not need to spend a lot of time on risk management, but you should do it seriously and out of conviction.

Those are only 10 points – and admittedly, they do require a bit of work. But I promise you that it's worth it!

Appendix

Web Sites of Interest

The Risk Doctor – http://www.risk-doctor.com/ (highly recommended)

PMI Risk Management Specific Interest Group http://www.risksig.com/

Software Engineering Institute - Carnegie Mellon, Risk & Opportunity Management http://www.sei.cmu.edu/risk/

All of the internet links in this book were current upon printing of this book in March 2013. However, it cannot be ruled out that some of them have changed in the meantime.

Recommended Books

Risk Management

Risk Management – Tricks of the Trade, Rita Mulcahy PMP, RMC Publications 2010

Practical Risk Management: The ATOM Methodology, Second Edition, David Hillson, Peter Simon, 2012

Identifying and Managing Project Risk: Essential Tools for Failure-Proofing Your Project, Tom Kendrick PMP, 2009

General Project Management

A Guide to the Project Management Body of Knowledge: PMBOK® Guide, Fifth Edition, 2013

About the Author

Roland Wanner has been in the project business for 19 years already and has seen lots of projects – some of them successful, others that have failed. After his education as a mechanical engineer and industrial engineer he spent 5 years as a project manager and after that several years as a project controller and project portfolio manager in mechanical engineering and construction. For more than 10 years he's worked as a project management specialist, project portfolio manager and project office manager in the banking and insurance sector.

Your Opinion is Important to Us!

Thank you for buying this book! We have done our best to ensure both quality content and design. Much effort was made to make this book as complete and correct as possible. However, it can't be ruled out that a mistake was made in one part of the book or another, whether contextual or grammatical. Maybe you think a certain piece of information is lacking or a certain subject should be expanded. We rely on your opinion!

We appreciate your ideas, thoughts and suggested corrections. Please send them to: info@pm-risk.com

Acknowledgments

With this first English Edition, I would like to thank the following for their unwavering support, trust and patience:

- My wonderful wife and my children, who gave me the moral support and time to write this book
- My editors and translators, especially Elisabeth Paregger and Elizabeth Stuart, who made this book as accurate as possible
- All the readers with their feedback and recommendations to make this and further books even better

Index

Appendix

Appendix

41031833R00068

Made in the USA
Middletown, DE
02 March 2017